GW00674624

THE
WORLD WAR I
AVIATOR'S POCKET MANUAL

THE
WORLD WAR I
AVIATOR'S POCKET MANUAL

Chris McNab

CASEMATE
Oxford & Philadelphia

Published in Great Britain and
the United States of America in 2018 by
CASEMATE PUBLISHERS
The Old Music Hall, 106–108 Cowley Road, Oxford OX4 1JE, UK
1950 Lawrence Road, Havertown, PA 19083, USA

© Casemate Publishers 2018

Hardback Edition: ISBN 978-1-61200-584-3
Digital Edition: ISBN 978-1-61200-585-0 (epub)

All rights reserved. No part of this book may be reproduced or transmitted in any form
or by any means, electronic or mechanical including photocopying, recording or by any
information storage and retrieval system, without permission from the publisher in writing.

A CIP record for this book is available from the British Library

Printed in the Czech Republic by FINIDR, s.r.o.

The information and advice contained in the documents in this book is solely for
historical interest and does not constitute advice. The publisher accepts no liability for the
consequences of following any of the advice in this book.

For a complete list of Casemate titles, please contact:

CASEMATE PUBLISHERS (UK)
Telephone (01865) 241249
Fax (01865) 794449
Email: casemate-uk@casematepublishers.co.uk
www.casematepublishers.co.uk

CASEMATE PUBLISHERS (US)
Telephone (610) 853-9131
Fax (610) 853-9146
Email: casemate@casematepublishers.com
www.casematepublishers.com

Cover design by Katie Gabriel Allen

CONTENTS

INTRODUCTION

Read any account of World War I aviators in battle, and it is almost impossible not to be humbled by the mental fortitude, physical resilience and exposed mortality of these young men aloft. Conditions for those flying high above the battlefields were scarcely imaginable to today's aviators, who as a rule operate within sealed, digitized and pressurised cockpits.

Back then, air crew sat in open cockpits, exposed to blinding direct sunlight or lethal winter cold, the latter accentuated by slipstream speeds of more than 160km/h (100mph). Flying through clouds soaked clothing and ghosted over the lenses of goggles; rain would drench not only the pilot but also his rudimentary flying controls. Physical protection was bulky and awkward. In the Royal Flying Corps (RFC) and Royal Naval Air Service (RNAS), the first clothing issued to pilots at the start of the war was basically the same as that given to Army motor transport drivers, although pilots could also purchase civilian flying jackets and other gear privately. A big jump forward came in 1917, with the introduction of the Sidcot suit, a one-piece layered and waterproof flying outfit that significantly increased body heat retention, the suit created by a former RNAS pilot. Electrically heated suits were even introduced towards the end of the war, as operational altitudes climbed as high as 5,500m (18,000ft), but these were only available in very limited numbers – the majority of air crew still relied upon layers of fur, leather, cloth and silk (silk scarves were worn around the neck to prevent neck chafing as the pilot constantly scanned the skies).

Whatever the clothing, the experience remained physically grim. Pilots would put on so much clothing before the flight that they might sweat profusely at ground level, the sweat then sucking away body heat when the man was aloft in temperatures as low as -50 degrees C (-58 degrees F). Wind chill would find the most minute cracks or gaps in clothing, sometimes inducing frostbite or hypothermia, or at least numbing limbs that desperately needed mobility to operate the aircraft controls. The face was particularly exposed. Aviators would often smear their faces with whale oil, then put on a balaclava helmet which was itself covered by a face mask, ideally made of non-absorbent fabric, including exotic materials such as Chinese Nuchwang dog-skin or Wolverine skin. Lips were treated with balm, although this rarely stopped them splitting open and bleeding profusely at altitude. At altitudes beyond 3,000m (10,000ft) the air crew were also at risk from hypoxia as the levels of oxygen dropped severely. Oxygen bottles and masks were provided, especially for high-altitude bombing crews, but many of the hardy aviators chose to ignore them, frustrated by the way that moisture in their breath often froze in and around the mask.

That human beings were able to fly, let alone fight, in such conditions is astonishing. And yet fight they did, in huge numbers and with equally huge losses. Depending on the phase of the war, the life expectancy of combat pilots was measured in days, not weeks – during the "Fokker Scourge" of 1916, for example, the typical life expectancy of an RFC combat pilot was just 17.5 hours' flying time. In total during the conflict, the UK lost nearly 35,970 aircraft, France 52,640 and Germany 27,640. Despite such attrition, the mental iron of the pilots is still apparent. One of them, Arthur Gould Lee, remembered "Yet the daily risk of a violent end was accepted unconcernedly. It was something we never spoke of and seldom consciously thought about. But for me it bred a hitherto unknown bond with other men – comradeship forged in the heat of dangers repeatedly shared." Such self-possession might not have been held by everyone – mental breakdowns were not uncommon – but the fact remained that men repeatedly climbed into cockpits when common sense implied that the aircraft were in effect little more than aerial coffins. Parachutes were rarely ever issued. Such pieces of kit were often deemed to show a lack of moral backbone, and it was felt that having a parachute might encourage aviators to take an easy way out of combat damage or mechanical problems, rather than working to their utmost to save a precious aircraft.

Note that a heavy share of losses, indeed the majority for nations such as Britain, were actually on account of mechanical failure and pilot error, rather than combat per se. For both aviation itself, and the process and practices of training military aviators, were very much in their infancy throughout World War I. Remember that the first controlled flight by a powered heavier-than-air aircraft – famously achieved by the Wright brothers – had only taken place on 17 December 1903, just a decade before the onset of war, and lasted just 10 seconds at a maximum altitude of 3m (10ft). Therefore, even with the enormous industry that aviation attracted, aircraft technology was still basic in the extreme by the time World War I began in 1914. The majority of the aircraft were biplanes, which were slower than monoplanes but offered better structural rigidity and manoeuvrability. Yet regardless of their type, size or purpose, most of these aircraft were lightly constructed of wooden struts, fabric coverings and tensioned wires. Such airframes were vulnerable to both battle damage and structural failure; pulling too tight a turn or too fast a dive could easily result in a loss of control or even an entire wing shearing off. Furthermore, understanding of both aircraft design and practical construction was still very much a work in progress; any errors in conception or assembly would usually only be revealed once a hapless pilot had taken the aircraft up. Aero engine technology was also a work in progress. Engine failures – particularly at altitude and in adverse weather conditions – were commonplace, possibly in the region of 5–7 per cent per plane, hence all pilots had to be trained in "dead stick" landings, although if a nice level field could not be found such landings often proved fatal.

Yet although the world of combat aviation – indeed aviation in general – was still very much new-born in 1914, the world's combatants pushed both the technology and tactics forward with gusto. At the beginning of the conflict, all the combatants had relatively small air forces – Germany had the largest air fleet, at roughly 250 aircraft, while France had 131 and the UK trailed behind, deploying only about 60 RFC aircraft to the frontline. The value of aircraft as instruments of combat was little recognized in 1914, but one area in which they could serve was in aerial reconnaissance, scanning the battlefield and enemy lines from an unimpeded vantage point. Aerial reconnaissance, both via balloons but more importantly with fixed-wing aircraft, was one of the early successes of the war, despite the severe limitations of communication technologies. (Before the advent of wireless communications later in the war, the observer of a reconnaissance aircraft would often simply create a sketch of the battlefront situation and drop it over HQ positions in a canister.) It was the intelligence provided by reconnaissance aircraft that helped the British Army give a good account of itself at Mons in August 1914, and which revealed the gaps between the German First and Second Armies the following September that led to the successful French counterattack on the Marne.

The first reconnaissance aircraft were generally plodding two-seater types, such as the Bristol BE2A. Its headline specifications were typical of the time – a 90hp engine delivering a maximum speed of 116km/h (72mph), a service ceiling of 3050m (10,560ft), a range of 320km (200 miles) – or endurance of 3 hours 15 minutes – and an agonising rate of climb of 325m/min (1,066ft/min). In the very first weeks, many of the reconnaissance aircraft were unarmed, opposing pilots either just acknowledging each other in the air with salutes or – as the serious tactical repercussions of aerial observation became clear – ineffective shots from a hand-held firearm.

It quickly became clear that more substantial armament was essential for both self-protection and for aggressive action. Two-seater aircraft acquired machine guns, typically a light machine gun on a flexible mount over the observer position. More significantly, a new breed of aircraft emerged – fighter aircraft – these being single-seat, faster and more manoeuvrable types purposely designed to interdict enemy reconnaissance aircraft and balloons. They were also required to have the capability of tackling other fighter aircraft.

Fighter aircraft proliferated in numbers and types from 1915, yet their development was constrained and shaped by the critical issue of weapon mount. To be an effective combat aircraft, the fighter aircraft needed a substantial primary weapon – ideally a heavy machine gun – which was aligned and fixed (not flexibly mounted) as far as possible with the pilot's line of sight. With a gun in this configuration, the aircraft was essentially turned into a flying weapon – when the aircraft was pointing directly at the target, so was the gun. The natural mounting position for such a weapon was the fuselage directly in front of the pilot, but there came the problem of how to shoot through a forward-mounted propeller. As a compromise, some early fighters had machine guns mounted on the top wing just above the pilot, the weapon shooting just above the arc of the propeller. The downside of this arrangement was that not only was the gun not directly aligned with the pilot's line of sight, but he also had an awkward time of things trying to load and fire the weapon, or clear jams. A different solution was actually to mount the propeller behind the engine and cockpit area, in a "pusher" configuration (i.e. pushing the aircraft from behind), leaving the front of the aircraft with an unobstructed field of fire. There were several fine examples of the pusher type fighters, one of the best being the British Airco DH.2, with its maximum speed of 150km/h (93mph) and single front-mounted 0.303in Lewis gun directly in front of the pilot. Yet pusher aircraft did not have the performance or manoeuvrability of "tractor" aircraft (i.e. aircraft with the propeller at the front, pulling forward). What was needed to create the new breed of fighter aircraft was a mechanical solution to mounting the forward-firing machine gun. Until this issue was solved, fighter aircraft could not excel.

One rather blunt solution was that adopted by French pilot Roland Garros in 1915, who, building on work already done by the French aero company Morane-Saulnier, fitted metal bullet deflector plates to the propeller blades. With these in place, a nose-mounted machine gun could be fired directly through the propeller arc, the majority of the rounds passing through the gaps between the blades while those that caught the blades ricocheted off the deflector plates. Garros' invention scored a small number of aerial victories when applied to a Morane-Saulnier Type L aircraft. But the invention was unsatisfactory on many levels, not least because it weakened the integrity of the propeller blades and caused the blades to spin less efficiently. The real breakthrough came with the "interrupter gear" or "synchronisation gear", which had been in various stages of independent development in France, Germany and Britain since 1913. The interrupter gear worked by synchronising the firing of the machine gun and the turn of the propeller through a mechanical linkage, meaning that the gun would only fire a round at moments when the bullet was guaranteed to pass safely through the gaps between the rotating blades. One of the first to implement this system successfully was Dutch-born German aircraft engineer Anthony Fokker, who built upon a design developed by Raymond Saulnier. Having developed a working synchronisation system using a belt-fed 7.92mm machine gun, Fokker allied the gun to a revolutionary new fighter, the Fokker *Eindecker* monoplane.

The introduction of the *Eindecker* – specifically in its E.III variant – in August 1915 began what amounted to a fighter aircraft arms race over the Western Front. In what was labelled the "Fokker Scourge", the E.IIIs inflicted punishing losses on Entente aircraft for a period of about five months. The weapon type and configuration, plus German innovations in squadron tactics and individual manoeuvres (such as the famous Immelmann turn, pioneered by fighter ace Max Immelman), for a time gave the Germans an undeniable air supremacy. Only the introduction of improved Entente fighters – principally the British F.E.2b/DH.2 and the French Nieuport 11 and, later, the Spad VIII – overcame the *Eindecker* threat in the first half of 1916.

From 1916, fighter aircraft evolved significantly, becoming more maneouvrable, faster and almost all armed with nose-mounted synchronised machine guns. Aircraft such as the Spad XIII, the Albatross D.III – which for a time in 1917 took an air superiority every bit as persausive as the Fokker Scourge – the Sopwith Camel and Royal Aircraft Factory S.E.5 were produced in huge volumes, and consolidated in large fighter-only formations. Fighter pilots became true gladiators of the skies, whose survival hinged upon their machines but most importantly their talent and daring as aviators. Furthermore, fighter aircraft also began to perform the ground-attack mission, conducted strafing and light bombing runs against ground targets. This evolved from an opportunistic role to a dedicated and formal part of air warfare, with entire units virtually dedicated to what we today call the close-air support (CAS) mission, integrated with large-scale battleplans. The Germans, for example, would send out entire 30-plane formations to perform multi-aircraft strikes at key ground targets in support of German infantry and artillery operations. Another critical role to emerge was that of aerial artillery forward observers, using the elevated platform and the first generations of wireless communications to adjust artillery fire onto target. But as the threat from the air increased, so land armies responded by, at first, canting the barrels of their small arms and artillery skywards, but then developing purpose-built anti-aircraft guns. Fighter pilots and ground-attack crews quickly learned that a low pass over the battlefield could be just as dangerous as a twisting dogfight high above the lines.

But alongside the nimble struggles of the fighter aircraft, there was another more cumbersome but equally important trend emerging in the history of combat aviation – strategic bombing. Strategic bombing – bombing raids against critical enemy industrial, transportation or civilian infrastructures – was actually conducted from the very outset of the war by German Zeppelin airships, which had exceptional capabilities in range and endurance (one Zeppelin, L59, flew for more than 6400km/4000 miles in 1917 without touching down once). Zeppelins conducted raids over both French and British cities throughout the war (although their primary use was aerial reconnaissance over the North Sea and Baltic), but it was clear by the end of 1916 that a combination of improved home-defence aircraft and better anti-aircraft defences left the huge and sloth-like Zeppelins horribly vulnerable. Moreover, fixed-wing long-range bombers steadily overtook airships as the main instruments of strategic bombing. These aircraft typically had a crew of between three and five men, with two or four engines. Some of the largest examples had capabilities that looked ahead to the heavy bombers of World War II. The British Handley Page V/1500, for example, had a nine-man crew, 4× Rolls-Royce Eagle VIII V-12 water cooled engines, a range of 2090km (1300 miles) and a bombload of up to 3400kg (7500lb). By 1917 all the major combatants had bomber fleets, attacking factories, rail stations, transport networks, troop concentrations and other influential targets.

Long-range aircraft also performed other critical roles, such as submarine hunting over the North Sea and eastern Atlantic as part of the RNAS.

Taking all the above trends and advances together, when it comes to aerial warfare what we see in World War I is a rather ad hoc but breakneck evolution. At the beginning of the war, aircraft were little more than a tiny, curious adjunct to the serious business of land warfare. By the end of the war, each side had air fleets numbering in the thousands of aircraft that actively contributed to every major campaign.

This evolution is reflected in the tone and content of the manuals presented in this volume. Although the manuals included, from a range of national sources, are rich in detail, there is often a distinct feeling that the authors are very much putting together the information on a month-by-month basis, responding to the constant shifts in technology, tactics and the course of the war. The dates on which the manuals were published are always revealing, the contents showing the current thinking or doctrine at a fleeting moment in time, as if caught in the flashgun of a camera before new developments come along. What we have here, therefore, is a tapestry of publications, issued as much to consolidate new thinking amongst aviators and their leaders as to provide definitive guidance.

CHAPTER I

DOCTRINE

Although the United States did not enter World War I until 1917, its military authorities naturally kept a close watch on technical, tactical and strategic developments in Europe, producing numerous military manuals in cooperation with or translation of European writers. *Military Aviation*, prepared by the War College Division, General Staff Corps, in November 1915 and published by the War Department, was a relatively short document that summarised both the current state of combat aircraft and the military structures in which they operated. The great value of this document is that it provides a superb snapshot of the aircraft types and tactics at this crucial moment in the war, at the end of a year in which fighter aircraft had rose to ascendancy. Nevertheless, we sense the writer striving for categorisations that do not yet exist with clarity. Hence fixed-wing aircraft are categorised as "(a) Scout or speed machines; (b) reconnaissance aeroplanes; (c) battle machines." Although this terminology would change quickly, the manual still provides us with a useful insight into how aviation doctrine was shaping up within both the European combat powers and within the watching US Army.

Military Aviation (November 1915)

II. GENERAL, TYPES OF AIRCRAFT.

4. CAPTIVE BALLOONS.

For over a century captive balloons have been used by the armies of all the leading military nations. Their function has been one of observation; that is, to see what those on the ground were unable to see. They have therefore proved a useful means of observing and reporting the effects of artillery fire. Electrical means of communication greatly enhanced the utility of captive balloons, as it made communication instantaneous from car to ground instead of by the older way of raising and lowering written messages by ropes. In clear weather and on favorable terrain captive balloons are able to distinguish different branches of the service at a distance of 16,000 yards or about 9 miles. With the best glasses at the present time the field of observation is said to extend to 20,000 yards.

In general, captive balloons of the "Sausage" or "Drachen" type are used by all the armies of the great nations. Along the French–German front in northern France these balloons are used in great numbers all along the lines. Their function is to observe the fire of artillery and keep watch of all movements of hostile parties within their field of view. They are connected by telephone directly with the batteries whose fire they are observing and with the headquarters to which they are attached. In many cases the captive balloons work in conjunction with aeroplanes. The aeroplanes by flying over the terrain where the hostile targets are located find out the exact position of those which the captive balloons have been unable to locate by themselves. When by means of signals the locations of the targets have been indicated to the observer in the captive balloon, the aeroplanes proceed to other duty.

Aside from the use of the captive balloons in conjunction with aeroplanes, their duties are practically the same as they have been for many years or were in our own Civil War. Free balloons such as were used from Paris, for instance, in 1870 are now a thing of the past, their place having been taken by the aeroplane or the dirigible airship. All military captive balloons are now so constructed that their undersurface acts like a kite, thereby making them steady in a strong wind. To keep the envelope distended properly in the face of the wind, a wind sail is provided so as to transmit pressure to the rear part of the envelope by means of the wind itself. Captive balloons are used not only with the field forces, but also are especially useful in fortress warfare. The organizations which handle these balloons consist ordinarily of some 4 officers, 72 men for each balloon section.

5. DIRIGIBLES.

The term *dirigible*, as applied to aeronautical appliances, signifies a lighter-than-air craft, which is equipped with engines and propellers capable of moving it from place to place. Dirigibles may be roughly divided into three classes: Nonrigid, or those whose envelope can be entirely packed into a small space when deflated, and that have no rigid framework of any kind; semirigid, or those that have a stiffening for a part of their length in order to enable the envelopes to maintain their shape to better advantage than the nonrigid; the rigid, which have a framework for the whole envelope that maintains itself continuously. All have been tried for the last 15 years. The nonrigid types have not given very good results, as they are too much dependent on the weather, due to distortion of the envelopes; the semirigid have given some satisfaction and have been largely employed. The advantage of the semirigid types is that they may be packed for shipment and reassembled much more easily than the rigid types; they can be deflated quickly and, consequently, are not so subject to complete destruction as the rigid types when anchored to the earth. On the other hand, they are not able to develop the speed that the rigid types, such as the "Zeppelin," are capable of.

Dirigibles and aeroplanes are frequently compared with each other as to their utility in general. As a matter of fact, they are two entirely different military accessories and are as different in many ways as is a captive balloon from an aeroplane. Dirigibles are able to stay in the air at any height for long periods of time. They are capable of running at reduced speed, can hover over localities for minute observation and to take photographs. They are able to carry several tons weight in addition to their passengers and crew. From the fact that they are able to remain stationary over a given place they are able to launch their projectiles with greater accuracy. Dirigibles in the present war have been used both over land and sea. At sea they have carried out reconnaissance, have acted offensively against hostile submarines, have accompanied transports in order to observe the approach of hostile craft, have been used in mine laying, stopping and examining hostile merchant vessels at sea, and for bombarding hostile localities. The airships which have made the longest trips and developed the greatest efficiency thus far are the German "Zeppelin" rigid-frame type. These have repeatedly flown over England at a distance of at least 300 miles from their base, and have nearly always returned in safety. Some have been lost, however. Aeroplanes appear to be unable to cope with them at night.

While dirigibles have not proved themselves to be a determining factor in combat, either on land or sea, they are being developed to the greatest extent possible, especially by the Germans, who have dirigibles of very great size. The principal features of this type are a rigid framework of aluminum, a number of drum-shaped gas bags, and a thin outer cover. Although the details of construction are not definitely known up to date, their length is about 485 feet, their volume about 900,000 cubic feet, their total lift over 20 tons, and their useful lift about 5 tons. They are driven by four motors of a total horsepower of about 800, which is applied to four propellers. Their speed is from 50 to 60 or more miles per hour and a full-speed endurance of over 100 hours, or more than 4 days. It is therefore evident that in good weather these airships have a radius of action from 5,000 to 6,000 miles. Moreover, they are being constantly improved, and are probably capable of crossing the Atlantic Ocean. Crews of from 10 to 20 men are required for their operation; they are armed with bombs of various sorts, light guns, and are equipped with searchlights. They carry very efficient radio apparati, which have equipments for determining the directions from which radio impulses are being sent. In this way they are able to locate themselves at night or in foggy weather when the ground is invisible. They require very large and expensive hangars, gas plants, and equipments for their operation. When forced to make landings outside of their hangars, on account of their bulk, they are very difficult to handle in hard winds, and are liable to destruction thereby.

The best of the nonrigid and semirigid airships have a capacity of more than 800,000 cubic feet, a maximum speed of 50 miles per hour or less, and a full speed endurance of about 24 hours. As mentioned above, their great asset is extreme portability and cheapness as compared with the rigid type.

6. AEROPLANES.

Heavier-than-air craft made their appearance as military agencies in 1908, when the Wright brothers demonstrated thoroughly their possibilities in this respect. While many of the salient features of heavier-than-air machines had been worked out years before, it remained for the internal-combustion engine to really make mechanical flight possible. The military possibilities of aircraft of this description were appreciated immediately by the great nations. Large appropriations were made at once, notably by France and Germany, for their development. At first England was slow to take up the matter, but in 1912 had gone at it thoroughly and was spending large amounts of money for their development. Italy, Russia, Japan, and the smaller nations of Europe and South America made liberal appropriations for obtaining the material and developing the personnel. Aeroplanes were used in a small way during the Italian campaign in Africa during the Balkan-Turkish War, and during the Balkan War. These nations had very little equipment and very few trained flyers. Wherever the aeroplanes were given the opportunity, under average conditions they rendered efficient service in reconnaissance.

7. TYPES OF AEROPLANES.

We now find aeroplanes consisting of three principal classes: (a) Scout or speed machines; (b) reconnaissance aeroplanes; (c) battle machines. The first are used for distant reconnaissance and combating the enemy's aircraft, the second for ordinary reconnaissance and the observation of fire of artillery, and the third for the destruction of enemy's material, personnel, or equipment.

8. REQUIREMENTS OF VARIOUS TYPES OF MACHINES.

Great advances have been made since the war began in all these machines, all the details of which are not yet available. The table on the following page, which appeared in the London *Times* of February 19, 1914, gives the approximate requirements of each type of machine at the beginning of the war. These general characteristics are still desired, but the radius of action and the speed have been considerably increased.

9. AEROPLANE ENGINES.

As to material, the most important consideration in aeroplane construction has been the engine. Without excellent engines the best aeroplanes otherwise are of no service; in fact, may be a source of danger. In the countries where aeroplane development has made the most progress large prizes have been given for the development of suitable engines. At the same time, research and experimentation have gone on along this line at Government plants. Engines require frequent replacement. In fact, it is reported that after 100 hours in the air engines are 'scrapped' and new ones installed. The plan found to give excellent results for the development of material is for the Government to have stations where experimentation along all lines is carried on. On the data furnished by these establishments specifications are made up for the construction of aircraft by private individuals and civil manufactures. If any

Performances required from various military types.

	Light scout.	Reconnaissance aeroplane. (a)	Reconnaissance aeroplane. (b)	Fighting aeroplane. (a)	Fighting aeroplane. (b)
Tankage to give an endurance of...	300 miles.	300 miles.	200 miles.	200 miles.	300 miles.
To carry...	Pilot only.	Pilot and observer plus 80 pounds for wireless equipment.	Pilot and observer plus 80 pounds for wireless equipment.	Pilot and gunner plus 300 pounds for gun and ammunition.	Pilot and gunner plus 100 pounds.
Range of speed...	50 to 85 miles per hour.	45 to 75 miles per hour.	35 to 60 miles per hour.	45 to 65 miles per hour.	45 to 75 miles per hour.
To climb 3,500 feet in...	5 minutes.	7 minutes.	10 minutes.	10 minutes.	8 minutes.
Miscellaneous qualities...	Capable of being started by the pilot single-handed.		To land over a 30-foot vertical obstacle and pull up within a distance of 100 yards from that obstacle, the wind not being more than 15 miles per hour. A very good view essential.	A clear field of fire in every direction up to 30° from the line of flight.	A clear field of fire in every direction up to 30° from the line of flight.

Instructional aeroplanes with an endurance of 150 miles will also be tested under special conditions; safety and ease of handling will be of first importance in this type.

Fig. 1.1

parts, such as the engines mentioned above, need additional development, prizes are offered to stimulate construction and progress.

III. FUNCTIONS OF AIRCRAFT.

10. HEIGHT AT WHICH AEROPLANES MUST FLY.

It was soon found out that to escape the fire of small arms a height of about 4,000 feet above the ground had to be maintained. As soon as balloon guns were created this height had to be increased to 6,000 feet, at which height it is now necessary to fly in order to be reasonably safe from being hit by hostile projectiles sufficient to bring the machine down. At this height, 6,000 feet, small details of the terrain and small detachments of troops or material are very difficult to distinguish. On the other hand, large columns of troops, trains, railways, bridges, artillery firing, and sometimes in position, defensive positions of large extent, and things of that nature can be readily distinguished. Whenever it becomes necessary for the aircraft to fly at a lower altitude than 6,000 feet the chance of destruction by gunfire must be considered.

11. STRATEGICAL RECONNAISSANCE.

Reconnaissance of this kind is strategical in its nature, the tactical reconnaissance of particular localities is still carried out by troops or captive balloons. In fact, it may be said that all strategical reconnaissance is now carried on by aircraft. The reconnaissance is carried out by an officer who requires considerable experience in order to be able to distinguish objects on the earth and assign to them their true military value. The pilot is either an officer or noncommissioned officer. The observer is always a trained tactical officer, because in reconnaissance of this nature an untrained person can not interpret the military significance of what he sees.

12. PHOTOGRAPHY FROM AEROPLANES.

Photography is utilized to the greatest extent possible in aerial reconnaissance. The devices are so arranged that they are capable of taking one or a series of views of a particular locality. The plates or films thus made are rapidly developed and are thrown on a screen by means of a stereopticon, when all details are magnified to any extent desired and details invisible to the naked eye are brought out plainly. These details are then entered on the maps of the officers concerned. As the height at which an aeroplane is flying can be taken from the barograph, and as the focal angle of the lens of the camera is known, a scale can easily be worked out and the views form good maps of the terrain photographed.

13. AEROPLANES AND ARTILLERY.

In addition to reconnaissance in general, aeroplanes have taken their place as a fixture for observing the fire of artillery. Due to the degree of concealment which artillery is now given, it is impossible to determine its location from the ground. The aeroplanes first pick up the targets, report their location to the field artillery, and then observe the fire of the batteries. By means of prearranged visual signals or radiotelegraph the aeroplanes are able to indicate to the artillery where their fire is making itself felt. If artillery is insufficiently provided with aeroplanes, it is well established that an enemy so provided has an overwhelming advantage.

14. CONTROL OF THE AIR.

For this reason, among others, attempts to gain "control of the air" are made by belligerents at the inception of hostilities. This takes the form of offensive action by aeroplane against aeroplane. For this purpose machines known as "speed scouts" and "battle aeroplanes" have been developed. All the great European nations are now equipped with them. The only way in which enemy aeroplanes can be effectively dealt with is by aeroplanes, because they are difficult targets for gunfire from the ground. To gain control of the air a great preponderance in number and efficiency of aircraft is necessary. So far in the European war, unless one side had a greatly preponderating number and quality of aeroplanes, they have been unable to obtain and keep control of the air. An excellent instance of obtaining control of the air seems to be furnished by the Austro-Germans when they initiated the campaign against the Russians in May, 1915. In this instance complete control of the air appears to have been obtained. The results to the Russians were disastrous because the Austro-Germans were able to fly at will wherever they wanted to, could pick up the location of the Russian masses, and make their movements accordingly, entirely unobserved by the Russians. In the fire of their artillery they had the advantage of being able to locate the Russian guns and observe their own fire, while the Russians were powerless to do so.

In an article on "Recent progress in military aeronautics," published in the Journal of the Franklin Institute for October, 1915, Lieut. Col. Samuel

Reber, Signal Corps, United States Army, sums up the question of machines for control of the air as follows:

> Experience has developed three types of aeroplanes for military purposes: The first, the speed scout, for strategical reconnaissance, a one seater, with a speed up to 85 miles per hour and radius of action of 300 miles and a fast climber, about 700 feet per minute; the second for general reconnaissance purposes with the same radius of action, carrying both pilot and observer and equipped with radiotelegraphy, slower in speed, about 70 miles per hour, and climbing about 500 feet per minute, and in some cases protected by armor; the third, or fighting craft, armored, and carries in addition to the pilot a rapid-fire gun and ammunition and so arranged as to have a clear field of view and fire in either direction up to 30 degrees from the line of flight, the speed to run from 45 to 65 miles per hour, and the machine to climb about 350 feet per minute.

15. SURPRISE MOVEMENTS.

It is often said that due to the use of aeroplanes surprises are no longer possible. Generally speaking, this is so, providing both sides are equally well equipped with machines and weather conditions are favorable. If, however, complete "command of the air" is obtained by one side, the chances of surprising the enemy are greater than they have ever been before.

16. BOMB DROPPING.

In addition to their functions of reconnaissance, the observation of the fire of artillery, and the combat of hostile machines, both heavier and lighter than air, much time, thought, and ingenuity have been given to the subject of dropping projectiles. Bombs of various sorts weighing from a couple of pounds to 50 pounds have been tried. The most common ones weigh from 15 to 35 pounds. At the height at which aeroplanes are required to fly it is extremely difficult to hit an object with any certainty. Various devices have been used and tried for this purpose. The factors of height, speed, and wind, are almost impossible to compensate for entirely, up to the present time, so that consequently bomb dropping in general or the launching of projectiles of all kinds from aeroplanes has not attained great results in so far as the actual destruction of material or personnel is concerned. Advances along this line are constantly being made, however, but progress is slow. A special type of aeroplane has been developed for dropping bombs and battle purposes.

For bomb attacks on any locality these machines are sent in flotillas of from 30 to 60 machines, each of which is provided with from 5 to 10 bombs. They go to the locality and circle over it, dropping their projectiles. Against railways, roads, bridges, and hostile parks of various kinds, this method of attack has given considerable success.

IV. ORGANIZATION OF AEROPLANE UNITS.

17. TACTICS OF AEROPLANES.

As to tactical use aeroplanes seem to be approaching methods similar to those used by a navy. That is, first the speed machines reconnoiter to the front; they are followed by the battle machines, which in their turn clear the way for the reconnaissance aeroplanes; those assigned to the artillery stay right with their guns. Fortresses, harbor-defense works, and naval formations require special organizations of aeroplanes, some or all of which may be operated from the water. The organization, kind, and number of the machines and personnel required for this particular service depend on the special locality and mission of whatever formation the aircraft are to be attached to.

18. DEVELOPMENT DURING EUROPEAN WAR.

The use of aeroplanes is gradually being developed from experience in the European war. Organization has been found to be one of the most important considerations; in general the organization has been into squadrons. The squadron is a tactical and administrative unit. It has a personnel consisting of pilots, observers, bomb droppers, mechanicians, chauffeurs, and drivers. Flying personnel has to be developed in the military service. Unlike chauffeurs, for instance, there are few in the civil population who can be drawn on. The few who fly are demonstrators, exhibition flyers, or sportsmen. They are very few in number and scarcely a military asset. In France the squadrons usually have six machines and two spares. They have the same organization of depots of resupply that other units of the armies possess. The squadrons usually consist of complete units of one kind of machine; that is, speed, reconnaissance, or fighting. These squadrons are usually assigned to an army, or more if the machines and personnel are available.

In general an aeroplane requires for its operation a personnel of 1 pilot, 1 observer, and 2 enlisted men, mechanicians, chauffeurs, etc. In England 12 machines of different classes are assigned to a squadron.

19. ASSIGNMENT OF AEROPLANES TO ARTILLERY.

Many are of the opinion that machines with the personnel to operate them should be assigned permanently to artillery regiments, so that they would be immediately available whenever action is required by the artillery. If they have to be obtained from a higher headquarters valuable time is often lost. It is believed that before long aeroplanes will be assigned permanently to regiments of artillery.

V. DEVELOPMENT OF AERONAUTIC PERSONNEL.

20. GENERAL LINE OF DEVELOPMENT IN EUROPE.

In the development of their aeronautical personnel all nations have worked more or less along similar lines. At first these detachments were attached to the engineers. All the pilots and observers were officers, while the mechanicians and others were enlisted men. As the science developed and more and more machines became necessary the importance of this branch constantly increased until eventually it formed a separate arm of the service. Instead of officers only being employed in the flying of the machines noncommissioned officers began to be used as the pilots.

21. OFFICER-OBSERVERS AND NONCOMMISSIONED OFFICER-PILOTS

The observers were either trained staff officers or officers of particular branches when the reconnaissance being made especially concerned a certain branch. For instance, in the observation of artillery fire an artillery officer, for the inspection of a demolished bridge over a great river an engineer officer, or for the observation of the tactical or strategical dispositions of an enemy's troops a staff officer. Noncommissioned officers are now very generally used as pilots. All countries now at war have found that they have places for all the trained pilots they can possibly obtain. In general the units are commanded by officers and a certain number of the pilots are officers, but the bulk of the piloting is done by enlisted men while the officers are carried as observers.

22. LOSSES TO AERO PERSONNEL IN WAR.

The losses to the flying personnel in war, when equipped with proper machines, seems to be less than that of infantry, cavalry, and artillery in the order named.

GROWTH OF THE RFC

Two years after the publication of *Military Aviation*, the British General Staff issued an internal military manual entitled *Offence versus Defence in the Air* (S.S. 188.J). It was again a short publication, but its purpose was primarily to explain to aviators and interested ground forces the evolution, structure and tactical rationale of both the RFC and the German air service. While such might not appear to be the typical content of practical manuals, the fact remained that military aviation was such a new and emerging topic that the fundamentals of how it had evolved needed explaining to the military populace. In the section reproduced below, the authors detail how the RFC developed in response to, and in leadership of, the new demands of combat flying over the Western Front. Note the passing point that in the early days "pilots occasionally threw out a few bombs in the course of their reconnaissance"; the author is being literal, as small bombs (often artillery shells or mortar bombs) were literally dangled over the side of the aircraft by hand and dropped.

Offence versus Defence in the Air (October 1917)

PART I.

THE R.F.C.

1.–Early Days.

The Royal Flying Corps, which accompanied the B.E.F. to France at the beginning of the war, consisted of four squadrons and one Aircraft Park, all under a single commander and working directly under G.H.Q. The Aircraft Park undertook the repair of aeroplanes and engines, and the supply and issue of stores and spare parts.

The squadrons consisted of a heterogeneous collection of all the machines available at the time, and squadrons, and even flights, were equipped with several different types of machine. The work of the R.F.C. consisted at first solely of reconnaissance, and aerial fighting only took place, and that very occasionally, as an incident of reconnaissance work. There was no idea of keeping machines, much less flights, for the primary purpose of fighting. Observers carried a rifle or an automatic pistol, but no aeroplanes carried a machine gun at this time A detailed scheme for co-operation with artillery had been worked out previous to the outbreak of war, but the system was in the early experimental stage, and very little artillery observation was done. Wireless had not been adapted to aerial work at this time, and observations were signalled by coloured lights, smoke bombs, or by movements of the machine.

Aerial photography was in its infancy, and although photographs of the German entrenchments were taken on the Aisne they were not regarded as of much interest. Bombing, as now understood, was non-existent, though pilots occasionally threw out a few bombs in the course of their reconnaissance. During the battle of the Aisne flights were attached to Corps, but were regarded as detachments from G.H.Q., whence they were controlled. As soon as the opposing forces settled down to trench warfare, the organization under one command was found to be too centralized and squadrons were definitely allotted to Corps. On the formation of Armies the squadrons with each Corps belonging to an Army were grouped into a Wing under the command of a Lieutenant-Colonel.

The expansion of the R.F.C. now began, and an additional squadron was formed at 48 hours' notice and despatched to Ostend to co-operate with the Antwerp expedition. One flight of special fighting machines arrived in October, 1914, and was assigned a purely defensive role, namely, to prevent hostile aerial reconnaissance.

As the R.F.C. grew larger and gradually took over more trench line, and as co-operation with the artillery became more systematised and more general, the need for further expansion became more and more apparent, and in the summer of 1915 it was decided that the following at last were necessary:—

One squadron to each Army Corps for artillery work and close reconnaissance, including photography.
One squadron per Army, and at least one for G.H.Q., for reconnaissance work.
One squadron per Army for special work, such as bombing raids.

Aerial fighting still took place on a minor scale only, but was gradually increasing, 26 fights taking place in May, 1915, 32 in June, and 47 in July. Many more than this often occur in one day in present conditions. It was already apparent, however, that fighting would be necessary on an ever-increasing scale to secure liberty of action for our artillery and photographic machines, and to interfere with similar work on the part of the enemy, and the need for the provision of purely fighting squadrons was realized.

The enemy's anti-aircraft guns had by the summer of 1915 become very troublesome, and the necessity for a large increase in our own A.A. artillery was also recognized. It is interesting to note that arrangements were made for co-operation between aeroplanes and infantry very much on the lines of the present contact patrol in connection with an attack south of Armentières in May, 1915. Little experience was gained, however, as the attack was not successful. By the autumn of 1915 the necessity of specialization had become still more apparent, and the division of the R.F.C. with each Army into two Wings was decided upon, one Wing for offensive action and reconnaissance, and the other for artillery work, trench reconnaissance and photography. A considerable increase to the number of G.H.Q. squadrons was also approved, and these were formed into a Wing early in 1916.

By this time the equipment of each squadron with a single type of machine had become general, but one or two single-seater fighting scouts were usually attached to Corps squadrons to provide escorts for artillery and photographic machines.

2.–The Development of Aerial Fighting.

From the beginning of 1916 onwards the expansion of the R.F.C. in France has been almost entirely governed by the development of aerial fighting. Artillery work, trench reconnaissance and photography, and contact patrol (introduced for the first time on the Somme) are still carried out by the one squadron allotted to each Corps, though the number of machines per squadron has been increased from 12 to 18, and is now being further increased to 24. The Army or offensive Wings and the G.H.Q. Wing have, on the other hand, become larger and larger, and are still increasing in size! Moreover, reconnaissance, at one time their principal if not their only duty, now fills a very minor place, aerial fighting absorbing the very great proportion of their energies. The first success in this struggle for superiority in the air was scored by the enemy, when he produced large numbers of single-seater fighting scouts of the Fokker type in the early spring of 1916, temporarily interfering to a considerable extent with the work of our Corps machines, and forcing us to carry out our reconnaissances with a number of machines flying in formation instead of with single machines as formerly. The need of more fighting squadrons, already realized, became more urgent, as did the necessity of faster types and better armament, and these conclusions were confirmed by the experience of the French at the battle of Verdun.

It was becoming increasingly evident that defensive measures cannot secure immunity from aerial attack. Owing to the unlimited space in the air, the difficulty one machine has in seeing another and the accidents of wind and cloud, it is impossible for aeroplanes, however powerful and mobile, however numerous and however skilful their pilots, to prevent determined opponents from reaching their objective, whether it be a machine engaged on artillery work, troops on the ground, or the target of a bombing raid. In the air even more than on the ground, the true defence lies in attack, and this was fully borne out, if further proof were needed, by the lessons learnt at Verdun.

At the beginning of the battle the French had few machines on the spot. A rapid concentration was made and a vigorous offensive policy adopted. The result was that superiority in the air was attained in a very short time and artillery and photographic machines were enabled to carry out their work with a large measure of immunity from interference.

As fresh units, which had less experience of working with aeroplanes, were put into the fight, a demand arose, however, for close protection. This demand was for a short time complied with. As a result the enemy resumed the offensive, and the French machines found themselves unable to prevent the raids which the enemy, no longer attacked himself, was able to make. The mistake was at once realized and promptly rectified. A general offensive policy was again adopted; the enemy's machines were kept so busy by constant attack that they were unable to undertake raids on their own account, and aerial superiority was once more gained.

Profiting by these lessons, every effort was made to increase the number of fighting and bombing squadrons in the R.F.C. prior to the Somme offensive, and immediately the battle started a policy of relentless and incessant offensive was pursued. The enemy had not as yet learnt his lesson. His Fokker machines were out of date and out-classed, and he had not yet provided anything to take their place. It is hardly too much to say that he was temporarily driven from the air, and the statements of many hundreds of prisoners showed to what extent his aviation was discredited among his own troops of other arms.

Drastic action was taken by the enemy. His systems of command and supply were re-organized, and he began to study and, on paper at all events, to copy our methods.

That such a regeneration of the German Flying Corps was inevitable had been recognised from the first, and an extensive programme of development was approved in the summer of 1916, and every endeavour made to place the R.F.C. in a position, when active operations commenced, in the spring of 1917, to continue and carry through the policy which had proved so successful. This programme contemplated a proportion of two fighting squadrons of the purely fighting type to each Corps squadron, a number of fighting reconnaissance squadrons, and at least ten squadrons specially designed for bombing. The extent to which the development of aerial fighting has governed the expansion of the R.F.C. will be realized if this programme is compared with the two or three scouts in each Corps squadron, which had been considered sufficient two years earlier, while even in the spring of 1916 the programme of expansion contemplated only two fighting reconnaissance squadrons and one purely fighting squadron in each Army Wing, with two fighting reconnaissance and three bombing squadrons grouped into a Wing under G.H.Q.

The experiences of the current year have fully borne out expectations. The enemy, too, made strenuous endeavour's to improve his relative position during the winter, and the amount of aerial fighting has increased by hundreds per cent. It has not so far proved possible to secure the measure of aerial superiority achieved in the early stages of the Somme battle, but the continual offensive action of the Army and G.H.Q. Wings, both by fighting and bombing, has enabled our Corps machines to accomplish a greatly increased amount of artillery and photographic work, and to work uninterruptedly and without undue interference every hour of every day that weather permits.

3.–Other Developments.

Apart from the fighting, the most important development as regards the employment of the R.F.C. has been in the direction of closer co-operation with the infantry. Contact patrol work was introduced at the beginning of the battle of the Somme, and has become a regular part of all active operations, both prior to an attack to reconnoitre the result of our artillery preparation and the state of the enemy's wire and other defences, and during an attack to keep those in command constantly informed as to its progress. Latterly, aeroplanes have taken a more immediate share in the infantry attack itself, actively co-operating by attacking the defending troops with machine gun fire from a low height, and by similarly attacking his reinforcements on their way to the battle front with machine gun and bomb. Further developments in this direction are almost certain.

CHAPTER 2
TRAINING AND CORE FLYING SKILLS

Training was one of the hot topics of early military aviation. The first combat aircraft, with their temperamental controls, fragile airframes and frequently erratic engines, were mechanically moody and difficult to fly. Unforgiving aircraft, combined with the lack of proper systematic air training in the early years of the war, meant that in most of the combatant air forces deaths from flying accidents were every bit as frequent as those suffered in combat. In the German Air Force, for example, a total of 1,080 trainee aviators killed in flying accidents alone, and this despite the fact that German training standards were actually generally higher than those of the British or the French. At the beginning of the war the RFC's trainee pilots passed through the Central Flying School, but this organisation was quickly overwhelmed by the exponential requirement for aviators. In response, the RFC created dozens of new training squadrons – more than 100 in number by the end of the war – and also sent new pilots to commandeered civilian training schools. Despite the apparent investment in training, the system was overstretched and haphazardly delivered, with some pilots going into combat with fewer than the required 15 hours of solo flying under their belts. That's if they made it into action at all. By the end of World War I, a total of 14,166 RFC aviators had been killed, but 8,000 of them had died while in training in the UK, an appalling total. Matters did improve by the end of the war, by which time the new Royal Air Force (RAF), formed from the RFC in April 1918, had implemented an 11-month flying course, with trainee pilots clocking up an average of 50 hours' solo flying time before being classified as ready for operations.

The manuals in this chapter, from British and American sources, perfectly illustrate the tactical and technical challenges of learning to fly in the early days of military aviation. The first of these manuals, the *Training Manual, Royal Flying Corps*, is from 1914, and thus provides an invaluable insight into the state of training at the onset of the war. It not only explains how the new aviator had to accustom himself to different aircraft types, but also the importance of that most critical of skills in those analogue days – navigation. Note, however, that the following sections only took up 13 pages of a 162-page manual, the rest of the book being devoted to the technicalities of aircraft and base procedures.

Training Manual, The Royal Flying Corps, Part 1 (Provisional) (1914)

CHAPTER VIII.–INSTRUCTION IN FLYING.

The precise methods to be adopted in instructing, and the time devoted to each detail, will vary with the circumstances of each case, depending on the type of aeroplane in use and the aptitude displayed by the pupil. Whatever the aeroplane, or whoever the pupil, the general principles of instruction, will, however, remain the same.

The preliminary instruction takes place inside the shed: The pupil is placed in the pilot's seat, and the methods of controlling the aeroplane and engine are explained to him. A rough idea as to why the various movements produce certain results is also given. The pupil then spends some time practising the movements, more especially trying to use his feet, hands and head at the same time. This part of the instruction should be discontinued when the pupil is quite familiarized with his surroundings and has a good grasp of what he will have to do in the air. If this instruction is unduly prolonged, bad habits may be formed, such as holding the control lever to one side.

Instruction in the air is now commenced. This should only take place in calm weather, as the pupil would become confused if a sudden gust or remous necessitated an abnormal use of the controls. Assuming the aeroplane to be fitted with dual controls, two or three flights, amounting in the total to about three quarters of an hour, at a height of about 150 or 200 ft., should be sufficient to enable the pupil to control the machine in calm weather clear of the ground.

The next stage of the instruction is the most difficult portion, i.e., teaching the landing. During the first few landings the pupil merely looks on and follows the motions of the instructor. After this he should be allowed to place his hands and feet on the controls. The instructor gradually allows him to control the machine more and more, until finally, possibly without being himself aware of the fact, the pupil carries out the whole operation unaided. This practice is carried on for some time, until the pupil makes the landing with complete confidence. The practice landings should be made at rather greater speed than the minimum flying speed of the machine, so that, when the pupil tries to reproduce this speed when alone, a slight error on either side will not be of much importance. It is, however, perhaps of value to occasionally do a slow speed landing (warning the pupil of the fact beforehand), so that, should he find himself in such a position that a slow speed landing is essential, he will have some idea of the extent to which the angle of incidence must be increased with a view to obtaining the right speed.

If there is no engine dual control, the pupil must next roll the machine on the ground for a few hundred yards, in order to get used to being alone in the machine and also to practise controlling the engine. Excessive rolling practice is not good. The pupil becomes accustomed to driving the machine while it is in an attitude which would probably be dangerous in the air. He may also lose his respect for the control levers, coarse movements of which produce little effect on the ground, but mean bad flying, and possible disaster in the air.

After the "rolling," the pupil proceeds to carry out straight flights exactly as he did with the instructor. Two or three such straights should suffice. He is then allowed to make two or three circuits, including both right and left hand turns. After this the instructor should take the pupil again and show him how to land without his engine from small heights.

All the flying instruction up to this point should have been carried out at a distance from the sheds or other obstructions; but now the pupil may be allowed to start from and return to the sheds in the ordinary way. During the instruction, the journeys to and from the sheds may be utilized to demonstrate the *vol plané* [gliding flight], and perhaps one or two fairly sharp turns may be done. A sharp turn is seldom necessary, but the pupil should be shown what it is like, in case he ever finds himself in such a position that it is necessary. There is the additional advantage that, when he comes to fly in something of a wind, he will have much more confidence in bringing the machine back from smaller angles than he has on previous occasions seen it brought back successfully.

It will be found that the mere taking of the Royal Aero Club certificate will instil great confidence in the pupil. At this stage any tendencies towards over-confidence should be at once checked.

After some further practice on the machine on which he has learnt, the pupil may be taught to fly a different type. One type or the other should now be selected, and the pupil should use no other until he has thoroughly mastered this one. Constant practice in flying is necessary, for in aviation, as in seamanship, good results can only be obtained after long experience.

The pupil must be warned that, under no ordinary circumstances, should any machine be brought down steeply with the engine "full out," for not only is the machine subjected to excessive stresses, but the controls may get so stiff that difficulty may be found in actuating them. Conversely, if the controls feel "sloppy," it is a sign that the speed is too slow, in which case the machine should be dipped for a few seconds with the engine running.

Notes on various types of machines. Maurice Farman.–This machine is peculiar in being almost the only modern machine to retain the front elevator (in types up to 1914). The Maurice Farman has a very good gliding angle, but not quite so good as is commonly supposed, for the reason that normally it carries its tail rather low, so that, during the glide, the machine may in reality be descending comparatively steeply, although the tail does not seem to be very high.

Many aeroplanes behave best in gusty weather, when a high speed is maintained; the Maurice Farman, however, is found to be most controllable at a speed of something less than its normal flying speed. Should bad gusts be met with at a certain altitude, and it is desired to come lower, the engine should be well throttled down on dipping.

Henry Farman.–The Henry Farman bears little resemblance to the Maurice Farman, except in details of construction and that the engine is behind the pilot.

In the air it is very quick in its movements. Whereas the Maurice Farman may be said to wallow when in a wind, the Henry Farman jumps about lightly. It is possessed of a considerable amount of natural stability, and, at the same time, the controls are powerful. It has more head resistance than most monoplanes or tractor biplanes, and so loses its speed quicker when the engine is cut off to land; also, the lifting tail plane has a slight tendency to drop when the slip stream from the propeller is removed. The elevator, however, is powerful, and this tendency is easily overcome. A good pilot can land it at a very slow speed, though not quite so slow as the Maurice Farman.

The passenger seat is a little in front of the centre of gravity, and a slight difference is noticed when a passenger is carried – the machine is better balanced.

A beginner should be warned not to make a sharp turn on this machine until he has had some practice, because the main planes are behind him and the bank may become excessive before he notices it. The pilot and passenger obtain a better view of the country than in any other type.

The Avro.–The Avro is a pleasant machine to fly. Only the outer part of the wing is warped, and thus the machine can be kept in good balance by adjusting the inner cells. The landing chassis is a very good design, and, while capable of standing very heavy shocks, does not bounce the machine up in the air if a slight pancake be made. The fore and aft control is sensitive, and the gliding angle very good. The rudder is also powerful, and banks the machine to a proper angle for turning, and, on this account, is useful also to help the lateral controls.

The B.E.–Is a tractor machine possessing a good range of speed, 70 to 40 m.p.h. It is capable of climbing, fully loaded, at a rate of 500 feet a minute.

The warping is controlled by lever, the steering by foot bar. The wings are flexible throughout and the whole of each wing warps.

The fore and aft control is light, but the lateral control is inclined to be heavy and apt to tire the pilot during a long flight in bad weather.

The flying angle of the planes is 3°, but with the warp they have a maximum angle of 10°.

The greatest efficiency is obtained at 4° or 5°, but the machine is flown at the smaller angle of 3°, so that a large surface is available for getting a big range of speed and rapid climbing. By reducing the angle of incidence towards the ends of the planes the self-warping effect is reduced and the pilot has to do more side control. The self-warping effect is most marked when the planes have the same angle of incidence throughout, but the machine is not so comfortable to fly.

Monoplanes.–Monoplanes generally are similar to handle to tractor biplanes. Though the maximum speed in both cases may be the same, the monoplane, having a smaller surface, cannot be landed so slowly, which is a great disadvantage. As a rule head resistance is cut down to a minimum, which is also a disadvantage when diving over obstacles to land in a confined space, since the speed becomes excessive.

A high-powered biplane can fly as fast as any practical monoplane, and has the enormous advantage of being able to go much slower. Of course a high-powered monoplane can be constructed to fly faster than a biplane, but it cannot be used except in very open country. The monoplane is more pleasant to fly, principally because the controls are lighter to the touch, and because of the absence of the feeling of being shut in.

CHAPTER IX.–NAVIGATION OF THE AIR BY DAY.

1. *General remarks.*–Accurate navigation is obtained by the intelligent use of a compass, combined with a good knowledge of topography to assist in rapidly locating the position. Great difficulty is experienced by pilots in finding their way across country at the first attempt, even if the locality is well known from below. The country presents a very different aspect when viewed from above, and only by constant practice can a pilot become what is known as a good cross country flier.

The secret of success in navigating an aeroplane is careful attention to details. The pilot's task is made considerably easier if he has a trained observer as passenger, with suitable means of communicating with the latter.

2. *Maps.*–Pilots must be well acquainted with map-reading. No map on a larger scale than 2 miles to an inch should be used for long flights; it is often impossible to use a larger scale than 4 miles to an inch.

It will sometimes be necessary in war to use foreign maps, the scale of which is usually given as a representative fraction. Pilots, when supplied with these maps, should immediately construct the corresponding English scale, i.e., so many miles to an inch. This will facilitate rapid calculation of distance in units pilots are accustomed to work with.

The pilot, having been directed to proceed to a certain point, or number of points, must closely study his map to ascertain what guides he can best use to assist his navigation. If there is no side wind, and his compass is correct, a straight course from point to point is the quickest. The points on the map should be joined by a line, and the "true" course measured. To this the variation (at Greenwich – 15° W.) must be applied, and he then has the compass, or magnetic course to be steered. The latter should be written down and kept in some conspicuous position in front of the pilot. The distances from the starting point should also be marked, either at 10-mile intervals, or from some well-defined object passed en route to the next. It should be noted whether any very high ground is to be passed over necessitating a greater height being maintained at that point.

3. *Selection of objects, &c., as guides.*–The following remarks are the result of practical experience :-

(a) Towns.–Towns are obviously of the greatest assistance. No aeroplane should, however, pass directly over them, as not only is such a practice contrary to law, but also, unless at over 2,000 ft., the effects of any large works

with blast furnaces, &c., will most certainly be felt. Towns should be clearly indicated on the map, either by underlining the name or by putting circles round them, so as to immediately catch the eye.

(b) Railways.–Railways are of very great assistance, and can be used to a large extent as a guide from point to point.

The conventional sign for a railway is a plain black line on the map, and no distinction is made between a line with perhaps four pairs of rails or one pair of rails. Thus it is quite easy to make a mistake, if a single line branches off from the main line in perhaps a not too conspicuous place. Branch lines to quarries, &c., are not often marked on the map, even though they may run a mile or more away from the main line. Tunnels, bridges and cuttings are marked on maps, and these will often be of assistance in picking up the correct line.

In spite of the above few details, which are liable to cause an error, a pilot should use railways whenever possible. He will find that, in windy weather when a course is perhaps difficult to steer correctly, and it is hard to allow for drift, it will be well worth his while to keep in sight of a railway, even if it takes him a little longer way round.

In such a case he should draw a line in the rough general direction of the railway and mark off its magnetic course. By comparing this with his compass, it will not only act as an assurance that he is following the correct railway, but it will also assist him should he become enveloped in a cloud or mist for a short time.

(c) Roads.–As a general rule roads are not a particularly good guide. There are so many of them in England which twist about considerably. Main roads are often less noticeable from a height than the minor roads. The telegraph wires and poles (a sure sign of an important road) are also very hard to see.

There are, however, exceptions to the main road rule. Roman roads, being usually absolutely straight, can generally be picked out easily, and also roads over a moor or plain, where there are few others in their vicinity with which to confuse them.

(d) Water.–Water can be seen from a great distance, and is a good guide. But after much rain a pilot must take into consideration the possibilities of a flooded stream causing the surrounding meadows, &c., to be inundated to a depth of perhaps only a few inches, but nevertheless having an appearance of a good sized lake or broad river, which cannot be located on the map.

Rivers are very winding, and are often almost concealed by high trees on either bank. A pilot will usually waste time if he elects to follow a river as a means of getting from point to point. On most maps the smallest rivers are marked very distinctly, which will at first encourage a pilot to follow them.

(e) High ground.–From a height of 2,000 ft. and over the country presents quite a flat appearance, and contour cannot be recognized. Nevertheless, the pilot should not fail to mark on his map any high ground with steep contours, as a warning that the landing is likely to be difficult, and as a reminder to fly high at this point.

(f) Forced landings.–Landing ground is hard to recognize as being good from a greater height than 1,000 ft. As it is usual to fly at somewhere about double this height, the aeroplane can glide for some distance before a spot is finally selected.

The best time of the year for flying is undoubtedly the autumn, when the crops are in. At this time a pilot should choose for preference a stubble field, which, from a height, presents a lightish brown appearance. By doing this he can be quite certain that the surface will be smooth, without ditches or mounds, whereas the ordinary grass field as often as not abounds in the latter. Dark green fields are usually found to be roots, and as such should be avoided, if better ground is available. Should a pilot land in a field of young wheat, &c., he will do well to get the first batch of sightseers to remove his machine to a corner of the field; this will prevent more damage to the crops than he has already caused.

(g) Wind.–Navigation would be comparatively easy if wind did not enter into the question. It is the more difficult to allow for, as it varies both in strength and direction at various heights. A side wind will cause an aeroplane to drift, that is to say, it will have to head up into the wind to a greater or less extent in order to remain actually travelling along the course required.

Should such a side wind be blowing when a pilot is about to start on a flight to a point some distance away, it will be quite worth his while to make a small diagram calculation, on his map to ascertain how much he should allow for it. This can be done in the following manner:–

A is the point of departure.
B is the point of destination.

Join AB (which should represent the magnetic course). From A (point of departure) draw a line down wind (i.e., with a S.W. wind the line would be N.E. from A). Estimate the speed of the wind (say, 20 m.p.h. at 2,000 ft.).

Speed of aeroplane 60 m.p.h. (say). This gives a ratio of 1 to 3 (speed of wind to speed of aeroplane).

Lay off 1 in. along the wind line from A, cutting this line at C. With centre C and radius 3 in., describe an arc cutting AB at D; join DC.

Then a line drawn parallel to DC through A will give the course that must be steered in order to reach B. The course in degrees can be found by measuring the angle BAW, and, in this case, adding to the angle thus formed 270°. Line AD will give the speed of the aeroplane relatively to the ground. Thus :-

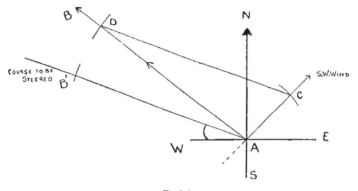

Fig 2.1

On starting off it is as well to circle while climbing, note the direction of the drift and pass directly over the point of departure. When directly over the point of departure, point the aeroplane on to her magnetic course and select some distant object on that course. Then head the machine up into the wind as necessary so as to pass over the object selected.

(h) Time.–The taking of times is often very much neglected, but nevertheless, it is an extremely important matter. In an aeroplane it is most difficult to estimate time. On calm days it seems to pass quickly, but on a rough journey the minutes pass very slowly; thus it often happens that a pilot who has not checked the time of passing some object expects to pass the next long before it is really due. From the commencement of a cross-country flight to the journey's end, the times at which the objects selected as guides are passed must therefore be checked.

(i) Height.–Over ordinary country, where there are no very high hills or mountains, a good height to keep at is from 1,500 to 2,000 ft. The presence of low-lying clouds, or of an unsteady wind, may necessitate a less or greater height, respectively, than those mentioned being kept. As a general rule, the

speed and steadiness of the wind increase as higher altitudes are reached, so that in making a flight down wind it may be sometimes more advantageous to fly higher than would be the case if the flight were being made, against the wind.

4. *Instruments*.–The following instruments should be fitted in an aeroplane intended for cross-country work:–

A properly adjusted compass.

A watch, preferably strapped to the pilot's arm. If fixed to the aeroplane without adequate means of preventing vibration, it will probably stop or not keep good time. An aneroid with adjustable height reading.

An engine revolution indicator. However skilled a pilot may be in detecting faulty running of his engine, after a long flight his hearing will not be so good, and an indicator will-assist him considerably.

A speed indicator, either in the form of a Pitot tube or a pressure plate instrument. This will indicate the speed of the machine through the air, and will be found invaluable when in a cloud, or when the ground is obscured from view by mist.

An inclinometer is required for ascertaining the angle of flight when the earth is not visible. For longitudinal angles the speed indicator is usually sufficient, as by noticing whether the speed is increasing or decreasing the pilot knows whether he is going "down" or "up."

A map board or case. For moderate distance flights, the pilot will find that a board placed in a conspicuous position will be quite sufficient to pin his map to; but for longer flights, he may find it necessary to cut his map into strips and use a roller map case. This method has the draw-back that consecutive courses, though perhaps differing considerably, will have to be drawn as if in a straight line. It thus requires a little practice for a pilot to adapt himself to its use.

QUALIFYING TO FLY

The *Textbook of Military Aeronautics* was an American publication, written in 1918 by aviation expert Henry Woodhouse, also the author of the *Textbook of Naval Aeronautics*. The stated purpose of the book was to "to make available to our prospective American aviators the educational information regarding the manner in which aviators fight the enemy", information gleaned "by talking to Allied officers and from the score or so of periodicals of the European countries engaged in this war". In the section given here, Woodhouse explains the qualifications and administrative requirements for various aviators' certificates in the United States, including those needed to pilot dirigibles. It also usefully outlines the US Army Preliminary Flying Test and US Army Reserve Military Aviator Test – it should be remembered that the US combat air service was embodied in the Aviation Section of the US Signal Corps. In the test descriptions, note the low altitudes of the manoeuvres. One of the reasons why there were so many training fatalities in World War I was that the low altitudes of the aircraft in training left almost no time for trainee pilots to sort out mechanical failures or flying errors before they hit the ground.

Textbook of Military Aeronautics (1918)

Tests for an Aviator's Certificate

In different stages of training the student or military aviator may go through tests and obtain the following certificates:

(1) The F. A. I. Certificate. This is the international certificate issued under the rules of the International Aeronautic Federation by the Aero Club

Fig 2.2 A group of students seated around a big relief map

of America. It represents the federation in the United States and in other countries on the American continent which do not have a national areo club affiliated with the International Aeronautic Federation. It is necessary to have this certificate to enter aeronautic meets, and to have records homologated and accepted by the International Aeronautic Federation.

Following are the rules under which F. A. I. certificates are granted by the Aero Club of America:

1. A person desiring a pilot's certificate must apply in writing to the Secretary of the Aero Club of America. He must state in his letter the date and place of his birth, and enclose therein two unmounted photographs of himself about 2¼ × 2½ inches, together with a fee of five dollars. In case the applicant is a naturalized citizen of the United States he must submit proof of naturalization.

2. On receipt of an application the Secretary will forward it promptly to the Contest Committee, which, in case of an application for an aviator's certificate, will designate a representative to supervise the test prescribed by the International Aeronautical Federation, and will advise the representative of the name and location of the applicant and, through the Secretary, advise the applicant of the appointment of the representative to take the test.

3. In case the application is for a spherical balloon or for a dirigible balloon pilot's certificate the applicant will be fully advised by the Contest Committee.

4. All applications for aviator's certificates must reach the Secretary a reasonable time in advance of the date that the applicant may expect to take the required test.

5. No telegraphic applications for certificates will be considered. Applicants for each class of certificate must be of the age of 18 years, and in the case of dirigible certificates 21 years, and must pass, to the satisfaction of the properly designated representatives of the Aero Club, the tests prescribed by the F. A. I., as follows:

Spherical Balloon Pilot's Certificate

Candidates must pass the following tests:

(A) Five ascensions without any conditions.

(B) An ascension of one hour's minimum duration undertaken by the candidate alone.

(C) A night ascension of two hours' minimum duration, comprised between the setting and the rising of the sun.

The issue of a certificate is always optional.

Dirigible Balloon Pilot's Certificate

Candidates must be 21 years of age. They must hold a spherical balloon pilot's certificate and furnish proof of having made twenty (20) flights in a dirigible balloon at different dates. They must also undergo a technical examination. In case, however, the candidate does not already possess a spherical balloon certificate, he must have made twenty-five (25) ascensions in dirigibles before he can apply for a certificate. The application for the certificate must be countersigned by two dirigible balloon pilots, who have been present at at least three of the departures and landings of the candidate.

The issue of the certificate is always optional.

Aviator's Certificate

1. Candidates must accomplish the three following tests, each being a separate flight:

A and B. Two distance flights, consisting of at least 5 kilometers (16,404 feet) each in a closed circuit, without touching the ground or water, the distance to be measured as described below.

C. One altitude flight, during which a height of at least 100 meters (328 feet) above the point of departure must be attained; the descent to be made from that height with the motor cut off. A barograph must be carried on the aeroplane in the altitude flight. The landing must be made in view of the observers, without restarting the motor.

2. The candidate must be alone in the aircraft during the three tests.

3. Starting from and landing on the water is only permitted in one of the tests A and B.

4. The course on which the aviator accomplishes tests A and B must be marked out by two posts or buoys situated not more than 500 meters (547 yards) apart.

5. The turns around the posts or buoys must be made alternately to the right and to the left, so that the flight will consist of an uninterrupted series of figures of 8.

6. The distance flown shall be reckoned as if in a straight line between the two posts or buoys.

7. The landing after the two distance flights in tests A and B shall be made:

(a) By stopping the motor at or before the moment of touching the ground or water;

(b) By bringing the aircraft to rest not more than 50 meters (164 feet) from a point indicated previously by the candidate.

8. All landings must be made in a normal manner, and the observers must report any irregularities. The issuance of the certificate is always optional. Official observers must be chosen from a list drawn up by the governing organization of each country.

Hydroaeroplane Pilot's Certificate

The tests to be successfully accomplished by candidates for this certificate are the same as those for an aviator's certificate, except that starting from and landing on the water is permitted in all of the tests.

United States Army Preliminary Flying Test

(a) Three sets of figures 8 around pylons 1600 feet apart. In making turns around pylons, all parts of machine will be kept within a circle whose radius is 800 feet.

(b) Stop motor at a minimum height of 300 feet and land, causing machine to come to rest within 150 feet of a previously designated point.

(c) An altitude test consisting of rising to a minimum height of 1000 feet.

(d) Glides with motor throttled, changing direction 90° to right and left.

Note.—(a) and (b) may be executed in one flight; (c) and (d) in one flight. The same rules apply in starting from and landing on water. Special attention will be paid to the character of landings made.

Report of these tests will be submitted to the officer in charge of the aviation section, with the information as to whether or not the school will complete the training of the aviator through the reserve military aviator stage.

If the preliminary flying test is passed satisfactorily and a candidate qualifies in other respects, he will be eligible for further instruction to qualify as a reserve military aviator.

United States Army Reserve Military Aviator Test

Reserve Military Aviator Test. The reserve military aviator test will be as follows:

(1) Climb out of a field 2000 feet square and attain 500 feet altitude, keeping all parts of machine inside of square during climb.

(2) Glides at normal angle, with motor throttled. Spirals to right and left. Change of direction in gliding.

(3) At 1000 feet cut off motor and land within 200 feet of a previously designated point.

(4) Land over an assumed obstacle 10 feet high and come to rest within 1500 feet from same.

(5) Cross-country triangular flight of 30 miles, passing over two previously designated points. Minimum altitude 2500 feet.

(6) Straight-away cross-country flight of 30 miles. Landing to be made at designated destination. Both outward and return flight at minimum altitude of 2500 feet.

(7) Fly for 45 minutes at an altitude of 4000 feet.

Any candidate who successfully passes the Reserve Military Aviator tests will, on application, be granted the "Expert Aviator" certificate by the Aero Club of America. An aviator desiring this certificate must apply in writing to the Secretary of the Aero Club of America, 297 Madison Avenue, New York City, sending the report of his R.M.A. tests, certified by the commanding officer of the school, by one of the officers who witnessed the tests, or by one of the officers of the administrative staff, together with the sum of $5.

The tests for the R.M.A. certificate are accepted in place of the club's own tests for the Expert Certificate. These are as follows:

1. A cross-country flight from a designated starting point to a point at least 25 miles distant, and return to the starting point without alighting.

2. A glide, without power, from a height of 2500 feet, coming to rest within 164 feet of a previously designated point, without the use of brakes.

3. A figure 8 around two marks 1640 feet apart. In making turns the aviator must keep all parts of his apparatus within semicircles of 164 feet radius from each turning mark as a center.

BASIC FLYING

The following excerpt is drawn from *Learning to fly in the U.S. Army; a manual of aviation practice*, another manual published just as the United States was entering war in Europe in 1917. The author, Professor E.N. Fales (US manual authors were often aviation academics, rather than combat-experienced pilots), explained that "With the sudden expansion of the Aviation Section of the U.S. Army since the declaration of a state of war with Germany, no book has been exactly suited to the aeronautic instruction of our 30,000 aviation students. These young men, called from non-technical occupations at short notice, must cram themselves in a few weeks with the gist of airplane flying, and must therefore omit everything except the outstanding fundamentals. The following pages set forth to the non-technical student aviator the gist of aviation, in such a manner that accuracy is not sacrificed to brevity." The picture painted of youthful fliers undergoing an inadvisably rapid acquisition of knowledge would be applicable to many European air forces as well. The value of the excerpt below is its accessible insight into the fundamentals of taking off and landing, typically two most dangerous phases of a flight for a pilot recruit.

Learning to fly in the U.S. Army; a manual of aviation practice (1917)

CHAPTER IV

FLYING THE AIRPLANE

Starting Off.–The first thing to do before starting off in an airplane is to inspect carefully everything about the machine and assure yourself that it is in perfect condition.

When all is ready to start turn the machine directly against the wind; this is done in order that the rise from the ground may be more quickly made with the assistance of the wind under the wings, and it has a more important advantage in the fact that if you try to get off the ground across the wind the machine will be very hard to balance. Birds also take the air directly against the wind even though for the moment this carries them in a direction toward some supposed enemy, and it is a fundamental principle in airdromes. Keep the machine pointed into the wind for the first 200 ft. of altitude (and similarly in landing face the wind when within 200 feet of the ground). In case the engine should fail before a height of 200 ft. is reached, never turn down wind as this is extremely dangerous.

Assistance will be had for the start from the mechanics, or if away from the airdrome from by-standers. Have each assistant in his proper place before starting the engine; one is to start the propeller and the rest to hold back the machine until ready to let go.

In order to get off the ground you will want good engine power; it takes considerable thrust to accelerate an airplane on the ground to its flying speed; in fact the first flying machine of the Wrights had to use an auxiliary catapult to furnish the thrust necessary to get them into the air. Making sure that the motor is giving full power raise the hand as a signal to the attendants to remove the chocks and let go. As you start rolling forward push the control lever forward which will raise the tail off the ground and place the wings edgewise to the wind while they will not offer resistance to the acquiring of good rolling speed. Within a few seconds the machine will have attained on the ground a velocity not less than the low flying speed; it will not rise, however, until the tail is lowered by pulling the lever back. When the necessary rolling speed is attained pull the lever softly backward; the tail at once drops, the wings increase their angle and lift and the machine will rise, the lever being held in a fixed position (see Fig 2.3). The distance between the point of starting and rising will be 100 yd. or more and will occupy from 5 to 10 sec. depending on the wind.

The change from flying position to climbing position is only a slight modification involving only a slight pulling back of the control lever and holding it in fixed position; the motor may in some machines simply be opened out when its increased power will make the machine rise; however, there is only one speed at which the climb will be fastest and therefore it is well to know what is the proper speed for climbing; the motor is then opened out full and the airplane operated to give the proper speed corresponding.

Fig 2.3 *(From "How to Instruct in Flying")*
Airplane in flying position just after starting.
This cut also illustrates proper landing attitude, since airplane is
just skimming the ground.

The pupil should rise to the height of at least 100 ft., as any less is useless and nothing will be learned from landing. In the case of cross-country flying the pilot will rise to the height of 2000 ft., circling over the field rather than flying off in a straight line so that preparatory to his start he always has the flying field in reach.

Landing. Proper landing is the most important thing in airplane flying. The pilot in turning his machine downward toward a landing spot from flight will choose a distance from the field equivalent to the proper gliding angle of his machine. If the gliding angle is 1 in 7 he must not turn downward any further from the field than a distance greater than seven times his altitude or he will fall short. It is safer to come closer to the field before turning downward for two reasons: first, because you may not be gliding at the best gliding angle; second, because you can always kill extra height by a spiral or two better than you can regain it. Have height to spare when landing.

Note that its attitude relative to line of flight is similar to "flying position," line of flight however being inclined.

To come down throttle down the engine and push the lever softly forward until the proper gliding angle is obtained (Fig. 2.4). The reason for throttling down the engine is: first, that you do not need its thrust when you are coasting down because gravity furnishes all the necessary velocity; second, if you glide or dive with the motor wide open high speed will result, resulting in strains on

Fig 2.4 *(From "How to Instruct in Flying")*
Airplane in gliding position, approaching a landing.

the machine especially on the moment of leveling out again; third, at this high speed the controls become stiff to operate.

Maintain the proper gliding speed to within 5 miles an hour of what it ought to be as it is the speed which determines the proper gliding angle. The revolution counter will indicate what the speed is or the air-speed meter may be used. Arrange to come on to the field facing directly into the wind, which may be observed by watching smoke or flags below. In landing against the wind you are again copying the practice of the birds. When you come to within 15 ft. of the ground pull the lever softly back until the machine is in its slow-flying position, which should be attained 5 ft. above the ground (Fig. 2.5). Hold the stick at this position of horizontal flying; no further movement of the lever is necessary except to correct bumps, for which purpose it would be held lightly for instant action.

The aileron control must be used here to keep the machine level and it may be necessary, to operate the rudder after touching the ground in order to avoid swerving; in fact some machines are provided with a rear skid which steers for this purpose.

In rolling just after landing keep the tail as close to the ground as possible without causing undue bumping, so that the maximum resistance of the wings may be presented to the air and the machine be slowed up rapidly. Some

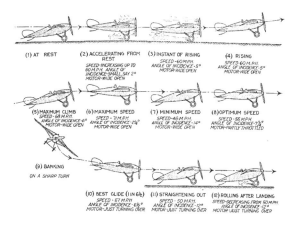

Fig 2.5 Attitudes of an airplane in flight.

machines are fitted with brakes on the wheels to assist in the quick retardation of the roll. Landing is one of the biggest problems in aviation and is a hard thing to learn because it is done at a high speed especially in the fast military machines such as the Fokker, Nieuport, etc. Landing is more of a problem than it used to be in the early days when, for instance, the Wrights were able to land without any wheels at all on mere skids because their machines were not fast.

The following are examples of bad landings:

1. The pancake results from allowing the machine to get into its rising position when it is landing (Fig. 2.6). There will be a perpendicular bounce and on the second bounce the running gear will break. In order to get out of an imminent pancake open up the engine to keep machine flying, put the machine into a flying position, then throttle down again and land.

2. Another type of pancake results from bringing the machine out of its gliding position at a point too far above the ground when the machine will drop due to lack of speed and break the running gear. To avoid this open motor full, thus regaining speed and flying position; afterward throttle down and reland.

Fig 2.6 *(From "How to Instruct in Flying")*
Bad landing, Type 1 – the "pancake" landing.
Line of flight is downward; angle of incidence large, hence speed is slow; but there is too much downward momentum and landing gear will break. Should line of flight arrow point upward, airplane as shown would then be in climbing position.

3. A third type of bad landing results from failure to turn the machine out of its glide at all, so that it glides straight downward until it touches the ground. This is the most dangerous case of all the bad landings. To cure it open up the engine after the first bounce, regaining flying speed before the second bounce; then reland.

4. If at the moment of landing the rudder is turned causing machine to swerve, or if the machine is not level, a side strain will be placed upon the landing gear and the wheels will buckle (Fig. 2.7).

Fig 2.7 *(From "How to Instruct in Flying")*
Bad landing Type 4 – machine not level.
Wheels do not touch ground at same time, and one may smash.

CHAPTER 3

AIRCRAFT ASSEMBLY, CARE AND REPAIR

Many of the aviation manuals written during World War I include chapters on flying and tactics but also detailed chapters on aircraft assembly and the fundamentals of aircraft engineering. While combat squadrons certainly had their own engineering sections, dedicated to keeping the aircraft in good flying condition, it was also imperative that pilots themselves had a firm understanding of how their aircraft were put together and maintained. Improvisation was often at the heart of military aviation during the war, particularly in the first years of the conflict when facilities, airfields and equipment were often in short supply. Thus both air crew and ground crew had to be able to find creative solutions to engineering problems, which in turn necessitated a comprehensive insight into every aspect of the aircraft's construction functioning. This effort was complicated by the fact that aeronautical engineering in general was a nascent science. The knots in the very principles of flight itself were still being worked out during the World War I, hence aviation engineering was constantly adapting to new insights (both theoretical and derived from combat experience) and the frequent introduction of new aircraft types.

Two manuals provide our sources for this chapter. The first is the *Training Manual, the Royal Flying Corps* (1914), already encountered. It provided sage advice about the general care and maintenance not only of aircraft themselves, but also of the engineering spaces in which the work was done. Finally, *A Few Hints for the Flying Officer* demonstrates the importance of the pilot striking up a good, informed relationship with his ground crew, based on mutual respect and also the pilot's demonstrated knowledge of fundamental engineering principles.

Training Manual, The Royal Flying Corps (1914)

CHAPTER I.–CARE OF AEROPLANES.

1. *General.*–The endurance and air worthiness of aeroplanes largely depend upon the care which is spent upon them. Aeroplanes should not be exposed to extremes of heat and cold. However well seasoned the wood may be, if it is allowed to absorb moisture, it will invariably deteriorate. Sheds, therefore, should be kept dry, and, as far as possible, at an even temperature.

An aeroplane can never be too clean. Rust, mud, dust and superfluous oil must be at once removed when it returns to the sheds. Further, an aeroplane, once housed, must have its weight supported in such a manner that there is no strain on the flexible suspension of the wheels. In this connection it must be remembered that the supports should be placed in such a position that the main weight of the machine is directly over them. The best position is immediately under the points where the undercarriage struts meet the skids.

Before an aeroplane proceeds on a flight, and after its return, all parts, such as control and aileron wires, fabric, &c., must be thoroughly examined, and the least sign of wear in any part must be at once corrected. It is important to watch the wear of the control wires at points where they pass over pulleys or through fair leads. For a thorough examination it is necessary to remove the grease first. All engines must be thoroughly tested before flying and after any repairs, or overhaul, have been effected. Finally, once a week, a thorough examination must be made of all struts, internal bracing wires of fuselage, &c., with a view to checking any damage, or want of alignment.

If an aeroplane makes a forced descent, and has to be left in the open, it is important to guard against probable contingencies. The aeroplane must be placed in as sheltered a place as possible, such as a hollow, or under the lee of a hedge, facing the probable direction of the wind, and must be pegged down.

2. *Fabric.*-The following points must be understood by all:–

Fabric is protected from the damp by doping it with "emaillite." Oil deteriorates both fabric and proofing material and must at once be removed as far as possible. Portions of fabric, which are liable to get saturated with oil, will require more frequent doping than the remainder. It will also be necessary to examine the woodwork beneath the fabric. An aeroplane in fairly general use will require redoping every six months.

Holes in the fabric must be repaired at once. If the hole is small a strip of fabric can be stuck over the hole and doped. If the hole is large it will be necessary to sew the patch in.

3. *Woods*.—Although proofing materials, such as "emaillite" and "cellon," are commonly thought of in connection with fabric, it must be remembered that they also afford an excellent protection to wood from damp.

4. *Internal bracing wires*.—These must always be painted in the case of both main planes and fuselages. The colour of the paint should be light so as to show up any signs of rust.

5. *External bracing wires*.-All external bracing wires must be either painted or greased.

6. *Turnbuckles*.—These must be protected from rust by a light film of grease. They must have sufficient threads engaged consistent with safety, and must be locked.

7. *Tyres*.—Tyres are injured by oil and grease. If they come in contact with such substances they must be at once cleaned. Pools of oil, therefore, must not be allowed to remain on the floors of sheds. Tyres should always be properly pumped up.

8. *Engines*.—Engines must be protected, whenever possible, by means of canvas covers which should be specially made to fit. Electric cables must be fitted so that the insulating material will not be exposed to damage either by excessive heat or by chafing against some sharp edge of wood or metal. Long lengths of unsupported cables are bad and should be avoided.

9. *Propellers*.—Propellers must be protected in the same way, as exposure to damp renders them liable to warp. As soon as flying is finished propellers must be wiped over.

10. *Bolts and nuts*.—Must be properly tightened up and locked by means of split pins or by burring the threads.

11. *Logs*.—Rough lugs kept in each flight. in which all details of flights, overhauls, repairs, expenditure of fuel and oil, &c., are entered at the time the casualty occurs, are of assistance in making the fair logs an accurate history of the aeroplane and engine.

CHAPTER II.–CARE OF AEROPLANE SHEDS.

1. *General.*–All aeroplane sheds must be kept free from dirt. Broken parts of aeroplanes or engines must not be left lying about, but must be separately stored until they can be repaired, or otherwise disposed of. Sound struts and similar parts must be kept together. Irrepairable parts must be at once turned over to the proper store, or otherwise struck off charge and disposed of in accordance with the orders in force.

Smoking in the sheds must be strictly prohibited.

2. *Floors.*–Floors must be kept clean by the application of hot water and caustic soda. Sawdust must not be allowed as it accumulates dirt–it is only permissible in a tray to catch the waste oil from the engines.

3. *Benches.*–When aeroplane sheds are provided with benches and vices, it is convenient that the benches should be fitted with "lock-up" drawers for the storage of tools.

4. *Tool boxes.*–Places should be allotted for the mechanics tool boxes and their contents must be periodically inspected. A list of the correct contents of a box should be pasted inside the lid.

5. *Trays.*–Every shed should have suitably partitioned trays for the reception of engine parts when engines are taken down for cleaning or repair. Parts of engines must never be left lying scattered about, or mixed with parts of other engines.

6. *Stands.*–Stands must be provided for engines to rest on when taken out of the aeroplanes.

If Gnome engines are used in the flight, it is advisable that a bench should be fixed in the shed to take the engine. This will facilitate timing, &c., before mounting the engine in the aeroplane.

7. *Clothing.*–Pegs must be provided for aviation clothing and helmets. No clothing should be allowed to lie about.

8. *Spare parts.*–Only the authorized spares may be kept in the sheds. The tendency to accumulate unauthorized spare parts must be checked. Care must be taken that spare parts, where applicable, are kept properly oiled or greased to prevent rust. Each part should bear a label showing exactly what it is and what it belongs to.

9. *Blow lamps.*–Blow lamps are not to be used except by authorized persons.

10. *Fire.*–Owing to the inflammable nature of the building, and the large value of the articles kept in it, every precaution must be taken against fire.

Fire alarms must be practised in flights at periodical intervals. Buckets of sand and water and hand pumps must be kept ready filled at convenient places in each shed. One petrol fire extinguisher, such as "Petrolex," should be kept in each shed ready for use, and all ranks should bow how to use this apparatus.

11. *Damp.*–Every precaution must be taken to guard against damp.

12. *Notice boards.*–A notice board should be provided in one of the sheds of each flight, on which, amongst other items, should be posted the name, address and relationship of the next-of-kin of every N.C.O. or man in the flight.

CHAPTER III.–REPAIR OF AEROPLANES AND ORGANIZA-TION OF WORKSHOPS.

The following has been found to be a suitable organization:–

1. *Personnel.*–The personnel available should be divided into three separate departments, with a serjeant [*sic*] in charge of each. The warrant officer should exercise general supervision over each department. The three departments are:-

(a) Aeroplanes; hull.

(b) Fabric work

(c) Engines, including blacksmith's, coppersmith's and welding work.

It is desirable that these departments should be located in separate buildings, but in small establishments this will not always be possible.

All mechanics must be made to realise that the greatest care and attention to the minutest details is absolutely necessary.

2. *Examination and dismantling of aeroplanes.*–This work, if it is made a matter of routine, is simple and occupies a small amount of time. The following is the system which has been found suitable:–

(a) In the case of serious damage or periodical overhaul, the aeroplane must be taken at once to the workshops by the men of the flight to which it belongs.

(b) The officer in charge of workshops then carries out his detailed examination, and prepares a statement, setting out in detail the general condition of the machine.

(c) The aeroplane is then stripped and all parts labelled.

(d) In all cases in which the machine has been in an accident the engine must be removed for a thorough examination and overhaul. For this purpose it must be handed over to the engine department.

(e) The parts which are not repairable are removed to the authorized place, and all small stores, such as turnbuckles, bolts, nuts, &c., which are apparently still serviceable are extracted and handed into the workshops store. In the store they are kept separate from the other spares until they have been pronounced serviceable, or otherwise, by the officer in charge.

(f) The parts which can be repaired and made fit for service are labelled, and sent to the department concerned where they will await their turn for repair.

(g) The undamaged parts are handed into the workshop store properly labelled. These should be taken on temporary charge as spare in the workshop store until the aeroplane is again ready for them. If the aeroplane cannot be repaired the undamaged parts must be taken on permanent charge in the store account of the unit.

(h) All instruments requiring repairs should be returned to store, and the officer in charge of workshops should decide whether the instruments are to be returned to the makers for repair or not. In the latter case a Board must be held and the instruments struck off charge.

(i) Any parts of the aeroplane which require further examination before a decision as to their serviceability can be given are labelled and stored neatly together, away from the remaining parts, until they can be examined.

(j) Before any repairable or sound parts are handed over to their respective departments, they should be thoroughly cleaned.

3. *Repair work.* (a) *Engines.*–A system must be established and worked on whenever an engine is taken down for repair and reassembled. Suitable stands must be provided on which to place the engines. Trays divided up into compartments, in which to put each part of the engine as it is removed, are a necessity. It is a good system to have each compartment numbered and the parts from each cylinder, and its attachments, put into that compartment corresponding to its number in the engine.

Only in cases of urgency should parts of one engine be used to complete another. If such a course is necessary, care must be taken that the parts so used are numbered afresh so as to correspond with the numbering of the engine in which they are to be used. Thus, if No. 5 piston of one engine is to be used as No. 7 of another, it should be re-numbered 7.

When reassembling an engine the utmost care is necessary to ensure that all the parts are absolutely clean and free from grit and dirt. Petrol baths are a necessity. Every part should also be thoroughly oiled before being replaced. Any metal part which has been bent should on no account be straightened and replaced in the engine without the knowledge of the officer in charge of workshops. As a general rule bent parts must not be straightened and used again.

(b) *Hull.*–Planes, while awaiting erection, must be properly supported on trestles. When the aeroplane is being erected all parts intended for that particular machine must be kept together so as to avoid using wrong parts.

(c) *Fabric.*–No fabric that has already been used once and doped can be used again for recovering another plane. Care must be taken to ensure that the fabric used is free from oil. Fabric workers should work in pairs. As far as possible the fabric shop should be kept warm and dry and at a constant temperature.

4. *Care of machinery.*–Only the mechanics authorized by the officer in charge of workshops should be allowed to use the lathes, saws, &c., with which the workshops are provided, and to start the motors for driving these machines. With electrically driven machinery, care must be taken that all switches are "off" before the shops are closed at the end of the day. Lathes, &c., and their accessory parts must be kept properly oiled and greased, and free from rust.

All belting must be provided with suitable guards. All flat-faced surfaces in lathes should be suitably protected by wood to prevent them from being damaged by tools falling on to them.

All shavings, sawdust, and metal turnings must be cleared away from the machines daily. The metal turnings should be preserved for future use or sale, different metals being kept separate.

5. *Stores and spare parts.*–No mechanic should be allowed an opportunity of making a private collection of spare parts for use in effecting repairs.

Pigeon holes should be provided for engine spare parts and various small stores, which should be labelled. Spare parts, where applicable, must be kept greased or oiled.

When drawing new parts from the store, mechanics should, as a general rule, and if possible, hand in at the same time the corresponding broken part. Broken or unserviceable parts must not be allowed to lie about; if they are, there is a possibility of their being used again by a careless workman. Condemned parts should be clearly marked (e.g., with deeply cut cross).

6. *Storage of spare planes.*–Spare planes should be stored in such a manner that their weight is evenly supported. One plane must not be allowed to butt against another. In this connection it has been found best to suspend planes by means of canvas slings hung from overhead. Within the loop of the slings there

must be a batten about 2½ inches wide. By this method the plane is supported evenly the whole way along.

7. *General remarks on organization.*—Workshops must be kept clean. At regular intervals, not less than once a week, all rubbish must be removed. Boxes should be provided in which waste metal, such as brass or steel turnings, may be kept. The benches must not be allowed to become mere shelves for an assortment of rubbish, spare parts and discarded breakages. No articles should be kept on a bench close to where some particular work is on hand, which has not a direct bearing on that work. When an engine has been overhauled and tested it should bear a label showing date of test, time run, and number of revolutions obtained. It should then be put to one side and greased, pending the necessity arising for its use in an aeroplane. Engines must be turned by hand daily. Log books should, if possible, be made up daily, the work actually done on each aeroplane or engine during the day being entered. Logs must invariably be made up to date, signed and forwarded at the same time as an engine or aeroplane leaves the charge of the officer in charge of workshops.

A Few Hints for the Flying Officer (no date)

1. The Flying Officer thinks, as a rule, that if he flies his machine, gives it a so-called air-test after a repair, and takes an occasional kit inspection, he is doing all he should, or could do, for the success of his Flight. This notion is wholly mischievous and wrong; his position carries with it certain quite definite ground duties, while it is on his attitude to his own work, on the standard he sets and insists on from mechanics working under him, and on his general interest in all the ground work of the Flight, that the maintenance of safe and serviceable machines chiefly, indeed almost entirely, depends.

2. A Flying Officer must have a thorough grasp of the general organisation and management of a Flight; names, trades, and qualities of all N.C.O.s and men, and machines in which they are detailed; outside size of a hangar in paces, and how the machines are disposed; number of principle spares held for a Flight, air-screws, planes, ailerons, axles, instruments, etc.; amount of its transport, and a clear idea of where everything should be stowed for a move; the breakdown routine and arrangements, with all personnel and gear carried; the correct way to make up logbooks and requisitions, with a clear idea of what are expendable and what are non-expendable stores; the time all principal repairs ought reasonable to take, renewal of shock-absorber, axle, under-carriage, bottom plane, air-screw, change of engine, etc. This is but a bare outline of

general organisation and management. There is needed in addition a knowledge of the methods of Flight work, besides all the technical information, and the practical knowledge and experience of the mechanics regarding the machines used. No mention is made here of the knowledge he should have, as an Officer of the personnel working under him, and of his duty towards them. No pilot who does not learn to treat his mechanics as an infantry officer treats, studies, and cares for his private soldiers, can ever hope to get good work out of them. A good Flying Officer must be a good officer as well as a good flier.

3. The only way to obtain the knowledge outlined above is to be present constantly in the sheds and with the machines. An Officer should go round the sheds every day; the men work the better, and feel that the Officers are taking an interest, both in them and in the progress of the work, which makes very much for good workmanship. At times also the Officer will be able to give a decision, or back up a young N.C.O., and in such ways help to speed up the work. He should notice what work is going on, how it is being done, quickly, systematically, and neatly, or with little progress and much fuss; whether the men at work have spread all spares, screws, nuts, tools, etc., tidily on a piece of fabric, or put them down casually on the cinders. Such points as these, even with the best mechanics, require the notice constantly of Officers. He should note who is taking the real lead in the work, and what actual share the N.C.O.s are doing themselves. One a wet day he should be careful to spend some time in the sheds. The whole Flight is apt to get slack and half-hearted, and every Officer should help to stiffen things up, and set an example of keenness in getting the machines put right. He should take this chance also for a more than usually thorough inspection of his own machine.

4. A pilot should always be present when any special work is being done on his own machine, e.g., at a change of engine, the weekly check-over, the fitting of a new axle or propeller. He should from time to time go and watch the work, find out if a test is wanted, and at what time, and he should be punctual. It is quite wrong to go off and leave instructions to send over to the Mess for him when he is wanted. It shows the wrong attitude.

5. When a pilot comes in late in the evening he should stay with the men while the machine is put away and the hangar closed down for the night, and should himself lend a hand. Similarly, when his machine is for an early flight, he should now and again get down to the sheds in time to help open up and bring the machine out. It is a chance for him, rare enough in R.A.F. work, to identify his own work and interests with those of the men, and it does a great deal of good.

When late night work is ordered he should go round during the evening just to show interest in the Flight. He should not stay, nor bother the men, who are anxious to get done with the work, but his visit is in a sense owing to the men, and will never pass unnoticed. It helps to keep them keen and cheerful.

6. A pilot should inspect his machine thoroughly every day, whether flown the previous day or not. It is quite wrong just to ask the mechanics. He should spend a quarter of an hour on it himself. He should find out when, and by whom, the tanks were filled, and see that the caps were properly screwed up and tested for pressure; pump up pressure himself, note that it is releasing at the right reading, that pressure holds up for some time, and that the hand pump is working correctly. He should try all taps and milled adjusting screws, both for leakage and easy working, examine petrol and other gauges for cracks and leakage, and try all controls. He should look at the belt fixings. Outside the machine he should note the condition of planes and ailerons, both for warping and tautness, struts and sockets for signs of splitting in the wood, wires for rust and tension; he should note if the shock-absorber, both of axle and tail-skid, is begging to stretch, of the axle to give, and if the wheels and propeller are clean. All should be done in a definite sequence, so that nothing is forgotten, and preferably when the mechanics are themselves cleaning down. There is nearly always something to bring to their notice. These daily inspections, if thorough, effect a marked and immediate improvement in the condition of the machines, and set a most valuable and necessary example of method and carefulness to the men.

7. A pilot should, of course, know the history and condition of his engine and machine. How many hours since last overhaul, size of jets, magneto advance, and when new leads and plugs were last fitted, petrol and oil consumption, general condition (hot or dirty, etc.), after a flight, if likely to oil up plugs, if an old, crashed, or new engine, etc., etc. He should know when the machine was last checked over, and how she was found, number of hours since planes, control and centre-section cables were renewed, etc. He should from time to time look through the Fair Log, and quite frequently go over mechanics' rough logs with them; mechanics often want keeping up to scratch in this respect.

8. When a machine is ordered out it is not right to wait until it is ready, and then walk over in flying kit and get in. It is far batter to go over and watch the handling of the machine out of the sheds, and all preparations. Men soon get slack and half asleep in handling machines, and it is an easy step from

this to actual careless work. N.C.O.s are never strict enough, and it needs an Officer to insist on all handling of machines being strictly and smartly carried out, exactly as a drill; as if a gun were being brought into action. He must insist on brisk, wide-awake behavior with aeroplanes at all times, and be careful to show it himself. The way machines are handled in and out of the sheds is a sure test of the quality of Flight workmanship throughout. To form these habits in the mechanic is perhaps the most important of a pilot's duties. It is never properly done by the N.C.O.s.

9. A pilot should assure himself that the machine is head in wind, chocks properly in place, airscrew not too greasy to hold, ground firm and not slippery. A question on such points shows that every detail is being strictly watched, and the men soon learn that details, with an aeroplane, are of vital importance. He must take care that his own orders and signals are quite clear, and that the men are constantly watching for them; that a mechanic takes his cap off to swing the propeller, and pays careful attention to the pilot's order "Switch off" before again touching the propeller after a failure to start; that there is no disorder or fuss when starting is troublesome, that chocks are smartly cleared right away, and that if a machine is slow to move the men do not "saw" at the wings, but allow the engine to do the work. The pilot should avoid shouting at men who get excited when handling a machine; it is mainly over-anxiety to please. A few quiet words after the Flight will do far more to encourage them. Getting an aeroplane out and away is just a complicated drill, and no "slap-dash" hurry or unnecessary talking should be allowed. The smartness of this drill mainly depends on the Flying Officer.

10. Before taking a machine up a pilot should *always* have a few words with the men, asking them some question about engine or machine, etc. It shows care for the work and interest in the men. He should make a point of showing them consideration in little things, making an effort to get the mud off his boots before getting in, not keeping them standing by for several minutes in cold weather, remembering to taxi slow when they are on the wings, to be patient and cheerful when they arrive up at the machine to restart the engine which he himself has lost in landing, to bring one of them back to the sheds in the passenger-sear, etc., etc. Such consideration in little things has an extremely good effect, far outweighing the little trouble it entails.

11. A pilot should always make a quick but careful scrutiny of the instruments, gauges, etc., on stepping into the machine. It is a great mistake to take a machine up hurriedly, without settling down and going to work carefully and methodically. He should try all controls, and when the engine

has been opened up should give a glance to the fitter. Besides being a safeguard, it is a chance to show an appreciation of his work, which is due to hun, and gives him something personal to work for. It is wise for a pilot to try in the air all the different pressure, petrol, and magneto systems separately, and to tell the fitter on returning that he has done so, the results to be entered in the rough log, as also maximum temperature shown, and extremes of oil pressure. It is quite rare to find all the systems working correctly, and only in this way can mechanics be taught to pay sufficient attention to them.

12. After a Flight a pilot should turn petrol off and tie up his controls himself. He should always have a few words with the mechanics, and say how he finds engine and machine, etc., no matter how cold and tired he may be. He should *never* simply go off without a word, fumbling for a cigarette. It is the only chance for the men to find out how the machine is flying; it is the time for him to point out the one or two details which *always* call for attention after a Flight, to see for himself if the engine is hot, etc., and to enquire what the mechanics are going to do to engine and machine. Moreover, after every successful Flight a pilot owes a word of praise to his mechanics. To pay it is to improve the relations between Officers and men, and to encourage good and careful workmanship. Not to pay it is at least an act of gross discourtesy. He should never bluff mechanics that something wants attention, unless he really thinks so, just in order to get extra examination of it. Mechanics always find the bluff out; it is taking unfair advantage of willing men, and very soon breaks their heart for the work. It is dishonest, and ruins all hope of confidence between Officers and men. It deserves and always gets a similar untruth in return. By attention to the points above an Officer is able to show his own scrupulous care where an aeroplane is concerned, and that nothing must be taken for granted or left to chance. It is an example never lost on mechanics; it is the only way to train up good ones.

13. The air-test of a machine is always a chance for an Officer to drill into mechanics the lesson of strict and careful workmanship. A test is not a joy-ride, but an important duty, to be carried out systematically like a drill. Before going up the pilot should ask exactly what was wrong, exactly what has been done, and why that should be the remedy, what definite points the men wanted noted in the air and who did the work. When he comes down he must go carefully and fully into the result. In this way mechanics learn to locate and correct fault methodically, to reason back to the cause of trouble, and not just to go to work at haphazard. This is the difference between good mechanics and bad ones.

14. When visiting another station a pilot must remember that his special personal care is essential if any work done on his machine is to be trusted. He must take a look around machine and engine himself. He should find out what experience the men have of this type of machine, and see that they understand what oil to use and how much to put in, how, if necessary, the radiator is to be emptied, etc., etc. He should state exactly what he wants done, if possible to a sergeant, and see that some show of starting the work is made before leaving the machine. Orders as to taking the machine in, filling up, etc., must be clearly understood. If the mechanics are unfamiliar with this type of machine he must see it handled into the shed himself, etc. This must all be done before anything else, before reporting arrival, or chatting to friends. Before going away explicit answers must be obtained as to how much petrol and oil has been put in, state plugs were in, whether pressure was tested after the caps were screwed down, etc. The pilot should assure himself as far as possible on all these points, and see that the mechanics clearly understand how the machine is to be started up. If any special work or repair is needed on the machine he should be with it throughout. He should never visit another station without his maps, even if the distance if both short and familiar to him.

15. When trouble is being located, or a failure to start, it is the pilot's duty to stand by until it is found, and becomes a matter of straightforward repair. The mechanics will have questions to ask him, and may want the engine run up, and he can help on the work very much by seeing that it is methodically carried out. This does *not* mean that he must walk up and down smoking, and ask the men every two minutes how long they will be. It is very bad for the mechanic to be chased and worried in this way, and to be made to feel he is working against time. Nothing is worse than having Officers hanging round a machine waiting impatiently until it can be got to work. A question or two as to what is thought to be wrong *and why*; how the fault is going to be traced, etc., will often prevent inexperienced men from just pottering about the machine aimlessly. It is an opportunity to stir up the initiative of young N.C.O.s to note likely men for promotion, and to insist on strict systematic working on machines. There is a way to do it without pestering the men.

CHAPTER 4
AIR-TO-AIR TACTICS

The skies over the battlefronts of World War I became history's first laboratories in aerial warfare tactics. More than anything, fighter tactics specifically were shaped by the general adoption of fixed forward-firing synchronised machine guns in 1915. From this moment onwards, the pilot's goal was to manoeuvre his aircraft into a direct-fire relationship with the opponent, who in turn attempted to evade the enemy attack and get himself into a shooting position. It was the birth of the fighter "dogfight".

The development of fighting combat tactics was evolutionary and communal. Many junior pilots, fresh to the front, had to glean as many combat tips as possible from local veterans before taking into the air. There were some manuals available – excerpts from which are reproduced here – but little in the way of a definitive and centralised corpus of knowledge. Instead, tactical recommendations were scattered in various forms amongst the fighting community, a process that included obtaining and translating enemy tactical documentation, if captured.

Another key source of tactical authority was that of the fighter aces, individuals – typically also in leadership positions – who had achieved high numbers of kills. Certain names stand out. On the German side, landmark figures are Oswald Boelke, Max Immelmann and Manfred von Richthofen (the "Red Baron"); for the French, René Fonck (who had the highest number of kills – 142 claims/75 confirmed – of any Allied fighter pilot) and Georges Guynemer; while Britain had luminaries such as Albert Ball and Edward "Mick" Mannock. Such individuals not only carved out reputations for themselves as individuals, many of them also helped to implement innovations in unit tactics, understanding that the chances of dogfight victories depended as much on inter-aircraft cooperation as personal flying skill. Some developed and published lists of "rules" for effective air fighting, these being pinned up on station notice boards and avidly digested by pilots eager to stay alive. Edward Mannock, for example, published a list of 15 rules in June 1915, when he became a flight commander. These still provide one of the finest summaries of tactical fighter combat best practice in World War I:

1. Pilots must dive to attack with zest, and must hold their fire until they get within one hundred yards of their target.

2. Achieve surprise by approaching from the East. *(From the German side of the front.)*

3. Utilise the sun's glare and clouds to achieve surprise.

4. Pilots must keep physically fit by exercise and the moderate use of stimulants.

5. Pilots must sight their guns and practise as much as possible as targets are normally fleeting.

6. Pilots must practise spotting machines in the air and recognising them at long range, and every aeroplane is to be treated as an enemy until it is certain it is not.

7. Pilots must learn where the enemy's blind spots are.

8. Scouts must be attacked from above and two-seaters from beneath their tails.

9. Pilots must practise quick turns, as this manoeuvre is more used than any other in a fight.

10. Pilot must practise judging distances in the air as these are very deceptive.

11. Decoys must be guarded against – a single enemy is often a decoy – therefore the air above should be searched before attacking.

12. If the day is sunny, machines should be turned with as little bank as possible, otherwise the sun glistening on the wings will give away their presence at a long range.

13. Pilots must keep turning in a dog fight and never fly straight except when firing.

14. Pilots must never, under any circumstances, dive away from an enemy, as he gives his opponent a non-deflection shot – bullets are faster than aeroplanes.

15. Pilots must keep their eye on their watches during patrols, and on the direction and strength of the wind.

Each point constitutes a hard-won lesson in fighter combat and survival. Yet even long experience was no talisman against mortality – of all the aces mentioned above, only one (René Fonck) actually survived the war.

Aeroplanes and Dirigibles (1915)

A duel in the clouds differs from any other form of encounter. It is fought mercilessly: there can be no question of quarter or surrender. The white flag is no protection, for the simple reason that science and mechanical ingenuity have failed, so far, to devise a means of taking an aeroplane in tow. The victor has no possible method of forcing the vanquished to the ground in his own territory except driving. If such a move be made there is the risk that the latter will take the advantage of a critical opportunity to effect his escape, or to turn the tables. For these reasons the fight is fought to a conclusive finish.

To aspire to success in these combats waged in the trackless blue, speed, initiative, and daring are essential. Success falls to the swift in every instance. An aeroplane travelling at a high speed, and pursuing an undulating or irregular trajectory is almost impossible to hit from the ground, as sighting is so extremely difficult. Sighting from another machine, which likewise is travelling rapidly, and pursuing an irregular path, is far more so. Unless the attacker can approach relatively closely to his enemy the possibility of hitting him is extremely remote. Rifle or gun-fire must be absolutely point blank.

When a marauding aeroplane is espied the attacking corsair immediately struggles for the strategical position, which is above his adversary. To fire upwards from one aeroplane at another is virtually impossible, at least with any degree of accuracy. The marksman is at a hopeless disadvantage. If the pilot be unaccompanied and entirely dependent upon his own resources he cannot hope to fire vertically above him, for the simple reason that in so doing he must relinquish control of his machine. A rifle cannot possibly be sighted under such conditions, inasmuch as it demands that the rifleman shall lean back so as to obtain control of his weapon and to bring it to bear upon his objective. Even if a long range Mauser or other automatic pistol of the latest type be employed, two hands are necessary for firing purposes, more particularly as, under such conditions, the machine, if not kept under control, is apt to lurch and pitch disconcertingly.

Even a colleague carried for the express purpose of aggression is handicapped. If he has a machine-gun, such as a Maxim or a mitrailleuse, it is almost out of the question to train it vertically. Its useful vertical training arc is probably limited to about 80 degrees, and at this elevation the gunner has to assume an extremely uncomfortable position, especially upon an aeroplane, where, under the best of circumstances, he is somewhat cramped.

On the other hand the man in the aeroplane above holds the dominating position. He is immediately above his adversary and firing may be carried out with facility. The conditions are wholly in his favour. Sighting and firing downwards, even if absolutely vertically, imposes the minimum physical effort, with the result that the marksman is able to bring a steadier aim upon his adversary. Even if the machine be carrying only the pilot, the latter is able to fire upon his enemy without necessarily releasing control of his motor, even for a moment.

If he is a skilled sharpshooter, and the exigencies demand, he can level, sight, and fire his weapon with one hand, while under such circumstances an automatic self-loading pistol can be trained upon the objective with the greatest ease. If the warplane be carrying a second person, acting as a gunner, the latter can maintain an effective rifle fusillade, and, at the same time, manipulate his machine-gun with no great effort, maintaining rifle fire until the pilot, by manoeuvring, can enable the mitrailleuse or Maxim to be used to the greatest advantage.

Hence the wonderful display of tactical operations when two hostile aeroplanes sight one another. The hunted at first endeavours to learn the turn of speed which his antagonist commands. If the latter is inferior, the pursued can either profit from his advantage and race away to safety, or at once begin to manoeuvre for position. If he is made of stern stuff, he attempts the latter feat without delay. The pursuer, if he realises that he is outclassed in pace, divines that his quarry will start climbing if he intends to show fight, so he begins to climb also.

Now success in this tactical move will accrue to the machine which possesses the finest climbing powers, and here again, of course, speed is certain to count. But, on the other hand, the prowess of the aviator — the human element once more — must not be ignored. The war has demonstrated very convincingly that the personal quality of the aviator often becomes the decisive factor.

A spirited contest in the air is one of the grimmest and most thrilling spectacles possible to conceive, and it displays the skill of the aviator in a striking manner. Daring sweeps, startling wheels, breathless vol-planes, and remarkable climbs are carried out. One wonders how the machine can possibly withstand the racking strains to which it is subjected. The average aeroplane demands space in which to describe a turn, and the wheel has to be manipulated carefully and dexterously, an operation requiring considerable judgment on the part of the helmsman.

But in an aerial duel discretion is flung to the winds. The pilot jambs his helm over in his keen struggle to gain the superior position, causing the machine to groan and almost to heel over. The stern stresses of war have served to reveal the perfection of the modern aeroplane together with the remarkable strength of its construction. In one or two instances, when a victor has come to earth, subsequent examination has revealed the enormous strains to which the aeroplane has been subjected. The machine has been distorted; wires have been broken — wires which have succumbed to the enormous stresses which have been imposed and have not been snapped by rifle fire. One well-known British airman, who was formerly a daring automobilist, confided to me that a fight in the air "is the finest reliability trial for an aeroplane that was ever devised!"

In these desperate struggles for aerial supremacy the one party endeavours to bring his opponent well within the point-blank range of his armament: the other on his part strives just as valiantly to keep well out of reach. The latter knows fully well that his opponent is at a serious disadvantage when beyond point-blank range, for the simple reason that in sighting the rifle or automatic pistol, it is difficult, if not impossible while aloft, to judge distances accurately, and to make the correct allowances for windage.

If, however, the dominating aviator is armed with a machine gun he occupies the superior position, because he can pour a steady hail of lead upon his enemy. The employment of such a weapon when the contest is being waged over friendly territory has many drawbacks. Damage is likely to be inflicted among innocent observers on the earth below; the airman is likely to bombard his friends. For this very reason promiscuous firing, in the hope of a lucky shot finding a billet in the hostile machine, is not practised. Both parties appear to reserve their fire until they have drawn within what may be described as fighting distance, otherwise point blank range, which may be anything up to 300 yards.

Some of the battles between the German and the French or British aeroplanes have been waged with a total disregard of the consequences. Both realise that one or the other must perish, and each is equally determined to triumph. It is doubtful whether the animosity between the opposing forces is manifested anywhere so acutely as in the air. In some instances the combat has commenced at 300 feet or so above the earth, and has been fought so desperately, the machines climbing and endeavouring to outmanoeuvre each other, that an altitude of over 5,000 feet has been attained before they have come to close grips.

The French aviator is nimble, and impetuous: the German aviator is daring, but slow in thought: the British airman is a master of strategy, quick in thought, and prepared to risk anything to achieve his end. The German airman is sent aloft to reconnoitre the enemy and to communicate his information to his headquarters. That is his assigned duty and he performs it mechanically, declining to fight, as the welfare of his colleagues below is considered to be of more vital importance than his personal superiority in an aerial contest. But if he is cornered he fights with a terrible and fatalistic desperation.

The bravery of the German airmen is appreciated by the Allies. The French flying-man, with his traditional love for individual combat, seeks and keenly enjoys a duel. The British airman regards such a contest as a mere incident in the round of duty, but willingly accepts the challenge when it is offered. It is this manifestation of what may be described as acquiescence in any development that enabled the British flying corps, although numerically inferior, to gain its mastery of the air so unostentatiously and yet so completely.

All things considered an aeroplane duel is regarded as a fairly equal combat. But what of a duel between an aeroplane and a dirigible? Which holds the advantage? This question has not been settled, at any rate conclusively, but it is generally conceded that up to a certain point the dirigible is superior. It certainly offers a huge and attractive target, but rifle fire at its prominent gas-bag is not going to cause much havoc. The punctures of the envelope may represent so many vents through which the gas within may effect a gradual escape, but considerable time must elapse before the effect of such a bombardment becomes pronounced in its result, unless the gas-bag is absolutely riddled with machine gun-fire, when descent must be accelerated.

On the other hand, it is to be presumed that the dirigible is armed. In this event it has a distinct advantage. It has a steady gun-platform enabling the weapons of offence to be trained more easily and an enhanced accuracy of fire to be obtained. In order to achieve success it is practically imperative that an aeroplane should obtain a position above the dirigible, but the latter can ascend in a much shorter space of time, because its ascent is vertical, whereas the aeroplane must describe a spiral in climbing. Under these circumstances it is relatively easy for the airship to outmanoeuvre the aeroplane in the vertical plane, and to hold the dominating position.

But even should the aeroplane obtain the upper position it is not regarded with fear. Some of the latest Zeppelins have a machine gun mounted upon the upper surface of the envelope, which can be trained through 360 degrees and elevated to about 80 degrees vertical. Owing to the steady gun platform offered it holds command in gun-fire, so that the aeroplane, unless the aviator is exceptionally daring, will not venture within the range of the dirigible. It is stated, however, that this upper gun has proved unsatisfactory, owing to the stresses and strains imposed upon the framework of the envelope of the Zeppelin during firing, and it has apparently been abandoned. The position, however, is still available for a sniper or sharpshooter.

The position in the sky between two such combatants is closely analogous to that of a torpedo boat and a Dreadnought. The latter, so long as it can keep the former at arm's, or rather gun's, distance is perfectly safe. The torpedo boat can only aspire to harass its enemy by buzzing around, hoping that a lucky opportunity will develop to enable it to rush in and to launch its torpedo. It is the same with the aeroplane when arrayed against a Zeppelin. It is the mosquito craft of the air.

How then can a heavier-than-air machine triumph over the unwieldy lighter-than-air antagonist? Two solutions are available. If it can get above the dirigible the aeroplane may bring about the dirigible's destruction by the successful launch of a bomb. The detonation of the latter would fire the hydrogen within the gas-bag or bags, in which event the airship would fall to earth a tangled wreck. Even if the airship were inflated with a non-inflammable gas — the Germans claim that their Zeppelins now are so inflated — the damage wrought by the bomb would be so severe as to destroy the airship's buoyancy, and it would be forced to the ground.

The alternative is very much more desperate. It involves ramming the dirigible. This is undoubtedly possible owing to the speed and facile control of the aeroplane, but whether the operation would be successful remains to be proved. The aeroplane would be faced with such a concentrated hostile fire as to menace its own existence — its forward rush would be frustrated by the dirigible just as a naval vessel parries the ramming tactics of an enemy by sinking the latter before she reaches her target, while if it did crash into the hull of the dirigible, tearing it to shreds, firing its gas, or destroying its equilibrium, both protagonists would perish in the fatal dive to earth. For this reason ramming in mid-air is not likely to be essayed except when the situation is desperate.

What happens when two aeroplanes meet in dire combat in mid-air and one is vanquished ? Does the unfortunate vessel drop to earth like a stone, or does it descend steadily and reach the ground uninjured? So far as actual experience has proved, either one of the foregoing contingencies may happen. In one such duel the German aeroplane was observed to start suddenly upon a vol-plane to the ground. Its descending flight carried it beyond the lines of the Allies into the territory of its friends. Both came to the conclusion that the aviator had effected his escape. But subsequent investigation revealed the fact that a lucky bullet from the Allies' aeroplane had lodged in the brain of the German pilot, killing him instantly. At the moment when Death overtook him the aviator had set his plane for the descent to the ground, and the machine came to earth in the manner of a glider.

But in other instances the descent has been far more tragic. The aeroplane, deprived of its motive power, has taken the deadly headlong dive to earth. It has struck the ground with terrific violence, burying its nose in the soil, showing incidentally that a flying machine is an indifferent plough, and has shattered itself, the debris soaked with the escaping fuel

Fig 4.1 *Alfieri*
Transporting a Belgian warplane to the aviation base in Northern France

becoming ignited. In any event, after such a fall the machine is certain to be a wreck. The motor may escape damage, in which event it is salvaged, the machine subsequently being purposely sacrificed to the flames, thereby rendering it no longer available to the enemy even if captured. In many instances the hostile fire has smashed some of the stays and wires, causing the aeroplane to lose its equilibrium, and sending it to earth in the manner of the proverbial stone, the aviators either being dashed to pieces or burned to death.

What are the vulnerable parts of the aeroplane? While the deliberate intention of either combatant is to put his antagonist hors de combat, the disablement of the machine may be achieved without necessarily killing or even seriously wounding the hostile airman. The prevailing type of aeroplane is highly susceptible to derangement: it is like a ship without armour plate protection. The objective of the antagonist is the motor or the fuel-tank, the vital parts of the machine, as much as the aviator seated within.

A well-planted shot, which upsets the mechanism of the engine, or a missile which perforates the fuel tank, thereby depriving the motor of its sustenance, will ensure victory as conclusively as the death of the aviator himself. Rifle fire can achieve either of these ends with little difficulty. Apart from these two nerve-centres, bombardment is not likely to effect the desired disablement, inasmuch as it cannot be rendered completely effective. The wings may be riddled like a sieve, but the equilibrium of the machine is not seriously imperilled thereby. Even many of the stays may be shot away, but bearing in mind the slender objective they offer, their destruction is likely to be due more to luck than judgment. On the other hand, the motor and fuel tank of the conventional machine offer attractive targets: both may be put out of action readily, and the disablement of the motive power of an enemy's craft, be it torpedo-boat, battleship, or aeroplane, immediately places the same at the assailant's mercy.

Nevertheless, of course, the disablement of the airman brings about the desired end very effectively. It deprives the driving force of its controling hand. The aeroplane becomes like a ship without a rudder: a vessel whose helmsman has been shot down. It is unmanageable, and likely to become the sport of the element in which it moves. It is for this reason that aviators have been urged to direct their fire upon the men and mechanism of a dirigible in the effort to put it out of action. An uncontrolled airship is more likely to meet with its doom than an aeroplane. The latter will inevitably glide to earth, possibly damaging itself seriously in the process, as events in the war have demonstrated, but a helpless airship at once becomes the sport of the wind, and anyone who has assisted, like myself, in the descent of a vessel charged with gas and floating in the air, can appreciate the difficulties experienced in landing. An uncontrolled Zeppelin, for instance, would inevitably pile up in a tangled twisted ruin if forced to descend in the manner of an ordinary balloon. Consequently the pilot of a dirigible realises to the full the imperative urgency of keeping beyond the point-blank fire of aerial mosquito craft.

The assiduity with which British aviators are prepared to swarm to the attack has been responsible for a display of commendable ingenuity on the part of the German airman. Nature has provided some of its creatures, such as the octopus, for instance, with the ways and means of baffling its pursuers. It emits dense clouds of inky fluid when disturbed, and is able to effect its escape under cover of this screen.

The German aviator has emulated the octopus. He carries not only explosive bombs but smoke balls as well. When he is pursued and he finds himself in danger of being overtaken, the Teuton aviator ignites these missiles and throws them overboard. The aeroplane becomes enveloped in a cloud of thick impenetrable smoke. It is useless to fire haphazard at the cloud, inasmuch as it does not necessarily cover the aviator. He probably has dashed out of the cloud in such a way as to put the screen between himself and his pursuer (Fig. 4.2).

In such tactics he has merely profited by a method which is practised freely upon the water. The torpedo boat flotilla when in danger of being overwhelmed by superior forces will throw off copious clouds of smoke. Under this cover it is able to steal away, trusting to the speed of the craft to carry them well beyond gunshot. The "smoke screen," as it is called, is an accepted and extensively practised ruse in naval strategy, and is now adopted by its mosquito colleagues of the air.

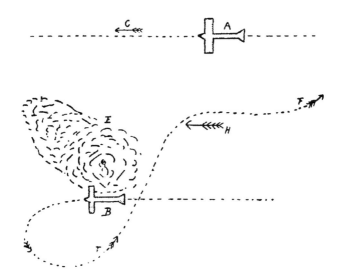

Fig 4.2 The "smoke screen" in the air.
B is being overhauled by A, both flying in direction H. B fires a smoke ball E, and under cover thereof doubles back, following route F, while A maintains his direction C. Under the cover of smoke B makes his escape.

FIREPOWER

The US manual *Practical Aviation* (1918) was, in its own words, "A text book for intensive study by men preparing to become skilled mechanicians and aviators, containing all the knowledge of fundamentals required prior to elementary and advanced flying." It was a large work, bringing together considerable knowledge of operational flying from the various combatants. In the passages reproduced below, there is detailed consideration of the firepower, mountings, ammunition and handling of aerial direct-fire weaponry. In the early days of the war, especially when the weapons were on flexible or wingtop mounts, the machine guns on the Entente side tended to be light, air-cooled and magazine-fed varieties such as the Lewis gun (explained in detail in the manual below). The Germans largely opted for the IMG 08, a lightened and again air-cooled version of the 7.92mm MG 08 heavy machine gun. The magazine-fed weapons had several constraints, not least the limited ammunition capacity compared to belt-fed guns, and the awkwardness of a magazine change during twisting manoeuvres. Thus fighters came to standardise on the belt-fed types, especially once the guns were set in a fixed forward-firing arrangement. Many of the machine guns mounted to fighter aircraft were variants of the Maxim machine gun, developed by Hiram Maxim at the tail-end of the previous century. The British and French, for example, relied heavily on the 0.303in Vickers, while the Germans maintained use of the IMG 08 or the MG 08/15. These guns had a cyclic rate of fire of around 550rpm, and an effective range of more than a mile, although the optimal engagement range in air combat was typically under 200m (219yds). The ball rounds from these weapons would easily shred aircraft fabric and struts, although sometimes would pass through the light bodywork without leaving critical damage. For this reason the prime targets were the enemy pilot himself and the engine, which could be readily set alight with tracer rounds. The close-range, open-cockpit nature of the warfare meant that pilots would often clearly witness the impact of their rounds on the opposing pilot's body; air combat in World War I was only notionally a gentleman's contest.

The first manual featured here, *Practical Aviation*, was a US Army Signal Corp publication produced in 1918. It collects extensive research about the use of machine guns in action and the core tactics of dogfight manoeuvres.

Practical Aviation, including construction and operation (1918)

FACTORS OF SUCCESS IN AIR COMBAT

Success in airplane fighting is not a matter of luck or due to the unreasoning type of dare-devil assault. Cool calculation and application of carefully defined principles of strategy and tactics is responsible for practically all victories.

The personal equation, always a great factor in success with arms, looms large in air combat. Aggressiveness must be combined with agility of mind and technical skill is of the utmost importance.

A third advantage rests with superiority in equipment, notably the speed, climbing and maneuvering ability of the airplane, its armor and the number and type of guns comprising its armament.

AIRPLANE SUPERIORITY

Engaged singly in combat, it is obvious that the advantage lies with the airplane which has the greatest mobility of movement, being enabled by superior speed, climb and flexibility to out-maneuver its opponent. The airworthiness, or flying qualities, determine which machine will emerge from circling and diving to the most favorable position, either above, below, in rear or advance of the enemy craft, advantages determined by tactical considerations such as type, armament, number and disposition of the hostile craft. Choice of position is largely governed by the type of airplane.

Tractors are ordinarily armed with two machine guns, operated either by the pilot or gunner, or both. With the pilot in the front seat, the gunner has a wide arc of fire to the rear, but with the pilot in the rear the gunner is in full observation and the machine is best maneuvered for direction of fire. Mounting the machine gun on the top plane permits operation from the rear seat; it therefore has obvious advantages. As combat airplanes are essentially of the pursuit type, the most effective fire should be to the front.

Pusher types are generally at a disadvantage because of inferior speed. But with the gunner placed well forward in the nacelle a wide arc of lateral and vertical fire is obtained. For heavier armament the pusher type has undoubted superiority, but in firing backward through the propeller efficiency is lost. Exception must be made in the double propeller pusher types where the arc of fire is clear, but although both tractor and pusher have separate advantages and both have many advocates, the speed and mobility of the tractor type give it a definite point of superiority.

STRATEGY

Familiarity with the appearance of various types of enemy airplanes, which is essential knowledge to the military aviator, includes an estimate of their speed and mobility, number, disposition and range of guns, and the best means of attacking in each case.

The former "blind spot," i.e., under the tail, is now defended by a machine gun which shoots through a tunnel in the fuselage; thus the approach from the rear, firing upward, is no longer a fundamental principle of attack. Clouds and the sun may be usefully employed; for to get between the enemy and the sun blurs the outline of the approaching plane. Hiding behind clouds and diving carries the element of surprise and is widely employed.

Acrobacy is an essential accomplishment, for a general rule governing air combat, in event of failure in surprise attack, is to duplicate every movement of the enemy engaged. If a diving attack is made the adversary dives, looping or zooming before the hostile machine guns are within range, thus reversing the position and gaining the altitude advantage. The same is true of climbing; the pursuer also climbs, attempting by superior climbing ability to reach a position where he can dive at his opponent. Short rises and dives in quick succession constitute an effective form of attack on a machine armed with two or more guns. Direct hits by machine gun fire are difficult of accomplishment and, due to the frequent misses, air combat remains largely a matter of skilful acrobacy. The operation of the airplane must be instinctive with the fighting aviator, aerial evolutions being accomplished without a second thought, so the greater concentration may be given to accuracy of fire.

Jamming of machine guns is frequent, often occurring at the crucial moment, and temporarily disarming the fighting pilot; a quick escape is then required. This can seldom be effected by straight-away flight at high speed toward friendly territory, owing to the target the machine will thus present. Side slips and spins, in fact all forms of aerobatics which give the appearance of an airplane falling out of control, are resorted to, the machine being straightened out when well out of range. At all times, therefore, the fighting aviator must know his position in reference to his own lines, for aerial combat may take him many miles within enemy territory. An aviator is ordered to take no chances when odds are against him, and strategy demands that an escape be attempted if anything goes wrong with his machine or gun.

THE LEWIS MACHINE GUN

This weapon is a standard airplane arm, weighing about 16 pounds, simple in action and with comparatively few parts. Success in its handling is largely dependent upon the operator's familiarity with the piece. The fighting aviator should have full knowledge of all parts of the gun and be able to dismount, assemble and adjust it without stopping to think about the process. To recognize, instantly, any fault in its operation while firing and to correct it without hesitation is, broadly speaking, the skill required.

GENERAL DESCRIPTION

The Lewis machine gun is air-cooled gas operated, and magazine-fed. The magazine is a circular drum in which the cartridges are arranged radially; the bullet ends are toward the center and are engaged by a spiral groove in the magazine center, down which the cartridges are driven until they are successively reached by the feed operating arm. While firing the other parts of the magazine are rotated about the center. Gas pressure, produced in the barrel by the exploding cartridge, furnishes the motive power for operating the mechanism. This gas, drawn into a cylinder through a hole near the muzzle of the barrel, drives a piston back, and thus winds the mainspring which operates the breach bolt and ejector, feeds a new cartridge, and rotates and locks the magazine. If the trigger is held back the firing is continuous until the magazine holding 100 cartridges has been emptied. To fire a single shot the trigger is pressed and released immediately.

OPERATING THE GUN

By constant reference to the drawing of the Lewis gun in section, Figure 4.3, the reader will understand its operation in detail from the following description:

Loading The charging handle (see slot at rear of 8-1 Rack on drawing) is placed in full forward position, the magazine placed on its post and pressed down, thumb piece of magazine latch to right. The charging handle is then

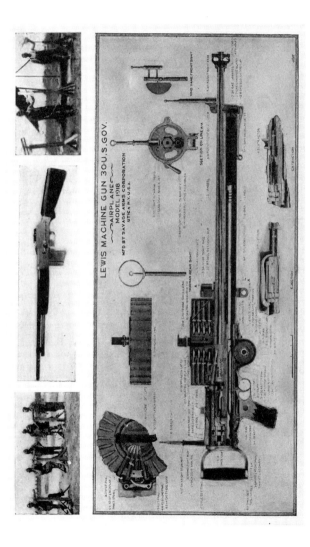

Fig 4.3 Sectional view of the Lewis machine gun, airplane model, assembled and beginning its loading operation; important parts of the mechanism are also shown enlarged. Above (left to right) military aviators in aiming drill; the light model Browning machine gun, which is belt-fed and the finest automatic rifle made; the targets used for aiming drills on the ground.

drawn back fully until it is engaged and held. This draws back the piston, drawing the rack teeth over the teeth of the gear (9-7) which rotates the gear and winds its mainspring. During the rearward travel, the striker (8-2) has been drawn back from the face of the bolt and the bolt rotated from right to left, turning the locking lugs out of their recesses. As the bolt is unlocked the striker post carries it back with it. The feed operating arm is swung across the top of the receiver by the feed operating stud (4-1); and the feed pawl (7-2), acting against one of the outer projections of the magazine pan, carries the magazine around sufficiently to drive the first cartridge down the spirally grooved center into the opening in the feed operating arm. This is the position pictured in the drawing, Figure 4.3. The feed operating arm brings the cartridge under control of the cartridge guide and a spring stud clears the stop pawl, which presses forward and prevents further rotation of the magazine. Meanwhile the rear end of the bolt has driven the ejector into its slot, and the rear end of the piston rack has set the sear spring which cocks the piece.

Firing When the trigger is pressed, the sear is drawn out of engagement with the notch in the rack, the latter being then drawn forward by the unwinding of the mainspring, rotating the gear in mesh with the rack.

In the forward motion of the bolt a stud cams the feed operating arm to the right, a spring stud on the latter pressing the stop pawl back from the magazine projection; the head of the bolt now presses the ejector into its cut and the face of the bolt, striking the base of the waiting cartridge, takes it from the loading ramps of the receiver and drives the cartridge into the chamber. The extractors spring over the rim as the cartridge seats. The bolt locking is completed by the forward motion of the striker post, which then enters the front part of its cut, carrying the striker against the cartridge primer and firing it.

The firing of the cartridge develops the power for another cycle of operation. As the gas which drives the bullet forward reaches near the muzzle of the barrel it is driven down through a hole into the gas chamber (J-34). Thence it passes under pressure through a hole, striking against the head or the piston and driving it back. This backward movement produces the movements of loading as described above. The empty shell, however, in the grip of the extractors is drawn back with the bolt, throwing the shell out of the ejector port.

If the trigger is held back the gun will fire again and continue the cycle of operations at the rate of about 10 shots per second until the magazine is empty.

ACCURACY AND VOLUME OF FIRE

Engagements between airplanes in combat are brief; thorough training in aiming and delivering machine gun fire is therefore given a prominent place in instructing the aviator. Gunnery skill is the deciding factor between opponents with equal technical advantages and flying ability, and at all times has considerable bearing upon victory or defeat.

ACCURACY OF FIRE

Due to aiming at a constantly moving target from a generally unstable base, accuracy in fire is seldom reduced to exactness. Distinct superiority in aiming may be acquired, however, by diligent practice on simulated moving airplanes, and is worth all the effort which may be given it.

VOLUME OF FIRE

High rate of fire is essential to an airplane arm, since the range is of limited length and the duration of effective fire reduced to a few seconds. The machine gun which operates at greatest rapidity and with smoothest action gives a decided advantage, owing to the limitations in accuracy of aiming.

FIRING AT GROUND TARGETS

Two types of targets are illustrated in Figure 4.4. In Figure 4.4a a circle of sand is shown with two intersecting ditches in the form and size of an airplane, filled with water so a splash registers a hit. An observer under cover watches and records the number of times the target is struck. The airplane illustrated has the gun mounted rigidly on the upper plane and the entire machine is aimed at the mark. A flexible cable connects the gun trigger to a lever on the control stick, the gun firing as the lever is squeezed. An open sight on a level with the pilot's eyes is used for aiming.

An advanced instruction device on the same principle utilizes a cross which revolves on a bar, describing a 40-foot circle. It is operated from a protected trench by means of a cable and pulley which rotates the target at the approximate speed of an airplane in a spiral. The shots are made at a height of about 800 feet above the ground.

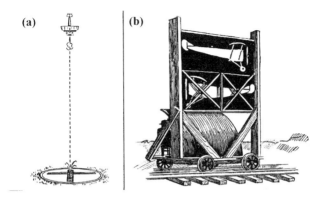

(a) **(b)**

Fig 4.4 a. The ditch target; a splash records a hit.
b. The moving target for ground practice, showing the armor shield for the operator.

Figure 4.4b clearly illustrates another form of moving target, the truck being operated by the man seated behind the armored shield. Students fire at the moving outlines of the airplane from the ground, either from a stationary seat or from the pivoted chassis shown in the photograph below, a representation of an airplane cock- pit which sways at the slightest movement.

AMMUNITION AND FIRE CORRECTION

Correction of machine gun fire is commonly made by observation of the path of phosphorous tracer bullets, placed about every fifth position in the magazine. The gun is deflected, raised, or aimed to either side, in accordance with the direction of the smoke trail toward the enemy airplane. The objective is usually the back of the pilot, aiming being governed by its appearance in the center of the sight. Various types of bullets are used in machine guns and an understanding of their functions and construction is useful.

TYPES OF AMMUNITION

The five common types of bullets for air warfare are illustrated in section in Figure 4.5a.

ORDINARY The head of this bullet is usually of solid brass and presents no new features.

PERFORATING This type of bullet is designed to pierce metal, being used against airplane motors and fuel tanks. The core is ordinarily of hard steel encased in a covering of copper, zinc and nickel alloy.

TRACING These bullets are hollow and filled with a phosphorous compound; the casing is, an alloy of copper, zinc and nickel. They leave a luminous or smoke trail behind and are combustible; they are designed both for fire correction and for incendiary purposes.

EXPLOSIVE The bullets are made somewhat in the form of a small shell; they are hollow and contain an explosive charge in the nose, consisting of chlorate of potash and sulphur, in equal parts, acting both as detonator and exploder. The lighter, flattened nose gives this type of bullets a different trajectory from those of ordinary form.

EXPANDING Destruction of struts and spars is the mission of the expanding type, drilled at the nose so instantaneous disintegration takes place even when encountering small diametered parts of low density.

CORRECTION OF FIRE

While several formulae have appeared to determine accuracy of aiming at hostile machines, practical application is well nigh impossible because they presuppose a knowledge of (a) speed of both airplanes, (b) aiming angle with reference to flight path, (c) enemy machine's flight path. The hopelessness of determining these is immediately apparent without proper instruments; dependence is therefore placed upon the trail of the tracer bullet, although special apparatus for sighting which makes an automatic correction has been developed, but must not be described just now.

A few principles of sighting upon which correction calculations are based are illustrated in the diagrams, Figures 4.5b, c and d. The only correction necessary in the case of Figure 4.5b is a raising or deflection of the gun or the airplane A, according to whether gun is fixed or movable.

In Figure 4.5c, enemy airplane B has a course at a wide angle to the path of A. Since the enemy machine is moving forward at high velocity, it is necessary to aim on the line A, C, the measure of correction being the line B, C.

Figure 4.5d illustrates the principle which depends upon the angle of the gun with reference to the flight path, it being necessary in this case to make

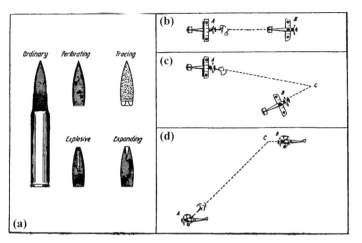

Fig 4.5 a. Types of bullets used in airplane machine guns for destruction and for correction of aim.
b. No correction laterally.
c. Lateral correction for velocity.
d. Longitudinal correction for velocity.

allowance for the forward motion of both machines, aiming at an approximate point C instead of directly at an enemy airplane B.

GUN MOUNTINGS AND FIRE RADIUS

Placing of machine guns and their number on enemy airplanes is a matter for exact knowledge with the military aviator. From recognition of a type he can estimate his chances of evading its fire and the best points of attack.

The various arrangements of armament of hostile airplanes becomes thoroughly familiar in sectors where daily engagements are the rule, and although distribution and number of machine guns are subject to constant change, acquaintance with the field of fire and mobility of the various arms establish certain principles which are fundamental and determine the possibilities of all modifications. Account must be taken of the value of surprise in arranging armament. A brief discussion of the effective fire secured by the various arrangements follows:

FORWARD GUN MOUNTINGS

The first consideration in placing forward guns in tractor types is their location. Figure 4.6ai illustrates the machine gun fixed to the upper plane and firing over the propeller; Figure 4.6aii gives the arrangement for firing through the propeller, as usually placed in one-man airplanes. Placing the gun on the top plane has two disadvantages: Resistance to the air, increasing the drift and consequently lessening lift, and difficulty in reloading the gun. To remove the empty magazine and replace it with a loaded one requires turning the gun upside down. When it is considered that the rate of fire is so rapid that the magazine is emptied in 10 or 15 seconds, it is obvious that unless a hit is made with the emptying of the first magazine the airplane is helpless in the matter of further immediate attack.

Shooting through the propeller is accomplished by synchronizing the discharge of the gun with the revolutions of the propeller, the mechanism being governed by the motor. The device is timed to suspend discharge when the blades are passing the muzzle of the gun; thus with a propeller revolving at the rate of 1400 r.p.m. the two blades pass that point at intervals of 1–47 of a second, a fraction of time which has no material bearing upon maintenance of virtually continuous fire.

Armoring the propeller blades to deflect the bullets is another method which has been employed, but is not favored to as great an extent as synchronizing. Triangular pieces of hard steel set in the blades at the point of the bullets' path save the propeller from breaking, under this method, and deflect the bullets striking them, the percentage of loss being negligible, as low as 5 to 8 per cent. Tapering the propeller at the point of the steel plate inset, however, means a loss in tractive efficiency, lessening airplane speed as much as 12 miles per hour, a consideration of so great importance as to make the method inferior to the synchronizing application.

EFFECTIVE ANGLES OF FIRE

The various arrangements of machine guns pictured on page 91 are worthy of careful study by the military aviator.

Figure 4.6b shows the application of a single forward gun to an airplane of pusher type, the weapon being pivoted in the front of the nacelle. The dotted lines show the limitations of the lateral and longitudinal arcs of effective fire, and the shaded portions the considerable dead area behind, the sides and rear being particular points of vulnerability.

Figure 4.6c illustrates the placing of a gun in the cockpit of a tractor machine, giving it a wider arc of effective fire to the sides and above and below,

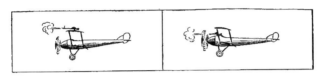

Fig 4.6a i. Gun fixed on upper plane.
ii. Firing through propeller.

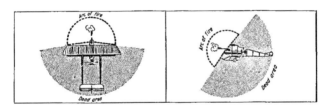

Fig 4.6b Lateral arc of single movable.
Longitudinal arc of single forward gun on pusher airplane
movable forward gun on pusher airplane.

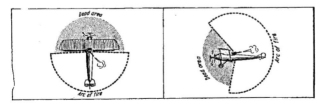

Fig 4.6c Effective lateral arc of rear gun.
Effective longitudinal arc of rear gun.

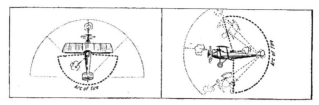

Fig 4.6d Arcs of forward fixed.
Longitudinal arc of fire with
movable rear gun same arrangement.

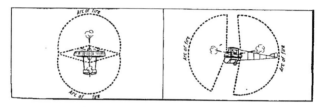

Fig 4.6e Joining arcs of two mobile guns.
Longitudinal radius of action.

but still leaving considerable dead area in front. The fact that this blind, or undefended, spot is in full view of the pilot who is maneuvering the machine makes it less vulnerable than in the case of Figure 4.6b.

Figure 4.6d shows the tractor airplane with the addition of a forward gun shooting through the propeller. The arc of fire of this gun is governed by the mobility of the airplane, that is, its radius of effective action depends upon the skill of the pilot and the machine's maneuvering ability in his hands, since the gun is pointed by the change of direction in the entire airplane. As this gun is mainly for offensives, the rear gun's function is principally defensive, a wide arc of fire to the rear enabling it to ward off attacks from many directions. This arrangement of guns is generally found on light bombing and reconnaissance or fire control machines.

Figure 4.6e illustrates the effective armament of either tractor or pusher types having two propellers. These machines are largely used for bombing and protection of aircraft or military bases, the armament being of great defensive value. Airplanes of this class with tractor screws are armed with the additional gun shooting through a tunnel under the fuselage already referred to. In type of machine many modifications appear, but this form of armament is general with practically all airplanes carrying three or more men.

FIGHTING IN THE AIR

Pilots of combat airplanes must be physically fit and mentally alert at all times. The enemy's qualifications for success are fully as great, and success is gained only by dauntless courage governed by quick-witted application of flying and gunnery skill. The following principles governing individual actions in combat are to be observed:

SKILL IN ATTACK

As in all forms of military science, surprise contributes largely to success. The surprise attack is best delivered from a position between the enemy craft and the sun. Diving on the tail is the favored method.

While diving, the rear should be watched; another enemy airplane may be above.

Except when coming to the assistance of friendly aircraft, speeds below 100 miles per hour should be employed, as excessive velocities make the airplane difficult of control and the period for machine gun fire too brief.

Fire should be withheld until within 100 yards of the enemy; the glove on the trigger hand is usually removed.

The machine on top has the advantage. Attack from behind is most effective; right angle fire is second choice, and attacking from in front the least effective method.

When the enemy airplane has superiority of speed the dive attack is used. If the hostile machine is inferior, the dive is made to his rear to a point a trifle below his tail; before opening fire flying speed is equalized by throttling the motor.

Careful survey of the sky should be made before attacking a single enemy airplane flying at a low altitude, as it may be a decoy.

The tail is the most vulnerable spot of the airplane; attacks may be delivered and expected most frequently at this point.

A one-man machine should not return to combat with a two-seater if the larger enemy craft has the position advantage when it opens fire.

When flying in formation superiority of numbers decides the advisability of attack; position in formation lost in combat should be regained at the earliest opportunity.

METHODS OF ATTACK

Figures 4.7 and 4.8a show some forms of air tactics in combat. Figure 4.7a illustrates a common method of support, airplane B remaining above clouds ready to assist airplane A which is engaged in combat with enemy E, or to attack any plane coming to the assistance of E.

Attack on an airplane which has encountered a hostile formation is illustrated in Figure 4.7b. The single enemy is surrounded and attacked from all sides, the leader of the formation remaining at a higher altitude and suddenly diving on his tail with a burst of machine gun fire. The method usually employed for attack on a single enemy by three airplanes flying in formation is shown in Figure 4.7c. Planes A B and C are discovered by enemy E, who immediately dives to escape. The leader A opens the attack by diving.

Fig 4.7a How a supporting airplane remains hidden from an attacking enemy.

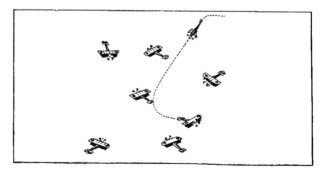

Fig 4.7b A formation engaging a single enemy, the leader taking higher altitude for surprise attack.

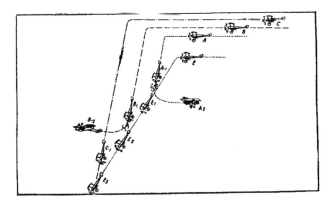

Fig 4.7c The usual method of formation attack on a single enemy.

Missing fire, he turns off to the left (path A1–A2). Airplane B, about 300 feet behind at slightly higher altitude, dives and fires; missing, he turns off right at B2, leaving the remaining plane of the formation C, in a steeper dive, to intercept the enemy at E3.

Attempted escape from a superior force by diving is seldom resorted to unless the lone machine has known superiority in diving speed. The usual method of getting away is by resort to air acrobatics, Figure 4.8b illustrating how the Immelman Turn can be successfully employed under the circumstances.

Figure 4.8a demonstrates the steeper diving angle required of the attacking airplane when the adversary is also diving.

FLYING IN FORMATION

Offensive combat in the air is seldom sought by a single airplane, well-defined and planned attacks against definite objectives generally being conducted by groups of machines, known variously by the terms wings, squadrons and fleets, according to their composition and numbers. The V-formation, illustrated in Figure 4.9, presents many advantages and is almost universally employed for air offensives.

In this arrangement the leader, who has the point and is in command, may keep all the machines easily under observation and his signals are

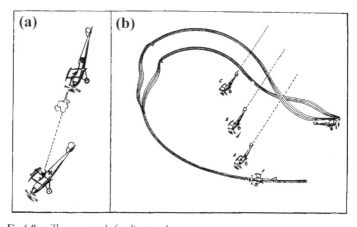

Fig 4.8 a. The steep angle for dive attack.
b. Employing the Immelman turn to effect an escape from an attack in formation.

Fig 4.9 An American squadron flying in V-formation.

seen without effort by all the pilots. The stations are determined in advance and each pilot takes his assigned position as close as possible to the other machines and slightly higher than the airplane immediately ahead. The formation is copied from the flight of birds, the aerodynamic reason for its adoption being that the air in the wake of an airplane has a downward motion unfavorable to flight, whereas the vertical character of the air stream to both sides of the leader has residuary upward motion. A military reason for the V preference over a possible diamond-shaped arrangement, is that in the latter three airplanes in the rear would be open to attack instead of two.

THE START

Upon the leader rests the responsibility of choosing pilots and machines suitable for flying in one formation. As a general rule it is important that each aviator take aloft an airplane with which he is entirely familiar. The machines and their pilots are assembled some minutes before the time set for the start, their clothing and equipment known to be proper for the mission, pilots seated and all engines running throttled down, before the leader takes to the air.

Once the leader is off the ground the other airplanes follow as near as possible in their formation order at intervals of 15 seconds. Attaining a height of 600 to 800 feet in straight-away flight, the leader throttles down and watches the others pick up formation. This should be accomplished at a maximum rate of about a half-minute per man. By rocking his airplane laterally, the leader then signals attention at night a red light is fired from a Very pistol and the climb is begun. If a turn is required to head in the direction of the objective, it is made in advance of the climb and before the motor is opened up.

THE FLIGHT

Constant watchfulness of the progress of his formation is required of the leader; he verifies the position of each airplane by looking around at intervals of one minute or less. The speed of the leader in climbing must be adjusted to the slowest airplane in the formation or the flight will be ragged from the beginning. Since speed is of paramount importance in air tactics, not only must the machines in formation be carefully selected for equal flying qualities but every pilot must hold his position with greatest possible exactness. Dropping out of place tends to slow up the progress of the entire formation and loss of position is for each individual a matter of grave importance.

Turning is done at a signal from the leader, who rocks his airplane repeatedly and pauses; he then turns in the desired direction in a small arc, throttling his engine and nosing down a trifle. Assume the turn to be to the right. The airplanes following on the right arm of the inverted V are throttled down and execute at slower speed a slight turn left, turning right when the leader has turned; meanwhile those on the left have successively made right turns with the motor on full. When all have turned the leader verifies the alignment and resumes full speed ahead.

Lateral rocking of the airplane is the attention signal.

Waving the arm and the direction it points indicates enemy aircraft.

The attention signal followed by rocking longitudinally signifies a machine gun jam.

While over hostile territory the difficulties of remaining in position are increased by anti-aircraft gunfire and the formation is often broken; but since success in attack is largely governed by the leader's freedom from concern about his force holding together, all pilots should regain position at the earliest moment. Constant vigilance should also be directed to preventing surprise attacks on the two rear airplanes.

EMPLOYMENT OF THE AIR FLEET

The plan of action is generally given to all pilots before a formation takes the air. Each man is expected to know his part in attainment of the objective and the leader's decision on the best method of attacking a hostile air force when sighted must be transmitted quickly by pre-arranged signals.

THEORY OF CONCENTRATION

Superiority of numbers is the general indication of the probability of success, although estimate of speed and armament of the enemy must be taken into account, along with the altitude advantage. Despite the growing tendency to the use of armor protection, mobility of action is thereby reduced and the upper position still remains a great tactical advantage. Lanchester, of the British Advisory Committee for Aeronautics, has evolved what he terms the N-Square Law, by which calculations on the probable chance of success may be reduced to mathematics. Application of the N-Square Law assumes equality in technical equipment, gunnery and individual airmanship, the fighting strength of opposing forces being then proportionate to the square of numerical strength multiplied by the fighting value of individual units. Two forces may be thus represented:

$$\begin{array}{rcl} \text{Enemy} = 10 \text{ airplanes, or } 10^2 & & 100 \\ \text{Friendly} = 8 \text{ airplanes, or } 8^2 & & \underline{64} \\ \text{Enemy's superiority} & & 36 \end{array}$$

The importance of superior tactics against the enemy is then shown by the assumption that the hostile formation is broken up, divided in half and attacked separately. The fighting value then appears:

$$\begin{array}{rcl} \text{Friendly} = 8 \text{ airplanes, or } 8^2 & & 64 \\ \text{Enemy} = 10 \text{ airplanes, or } 5^2 + 5^2 & & \underline{50} \\ \text{Friendly force's superiority} & & 14 \end{array}$$

While application of the N-Square Law may only reflect the probability of success in a theoretical way, similar mathematical calculations, its creator points out, have been used deliberately or unconsciously by great military leaders of the past.

While superiority in numbers in air warfare is the primary indication of success, the principles of aerial warfare demand an attack when there is the slightest chance of success, and perhaps more than in other military branches, a leader's tactical skill is the deciding factor in air combat.

WARFARE ALTITUDES

The importance of altitude, when previously mentioned, referred to securing the upper position when engaging an enemy. Flight altitudes should be considered from another viewpoint, i.e., the divisions of flying heights in accordance with the mission of the airplane. Set rules cannot be made on this score as altitude in warfare is influenced by the tactical situation and atmospheric conditions. A general classification divides flight levels into low, mean and high. Low altitude includes anything up to 5,000 feet; offensives against ground objective being conducted below 2,000 feet, and 2,500 to 3,000 feet being most favorable for night operations, bombing and photography. At mean height, 5,000 to 10,000 feet, combat planes have the most favorable altitude for tactical missions; photographic, fire-control and bombing machines may also employ these elevations. High flight, 10,000 feet and above, appears best suited for combat airplanes in the aircraft screen and those seeking to avoid hostile craft when proceeding on or returning from a mission.

TACTICAL SKILL

Essentially, military airplanes are fighting units, not individuals, and should operate in groups or formations, the strength and composition of which are governed by the nature of the mission. Operating singly, the duties assigned should be those which permit the craft to remain within areas providing support from other aircraft.

Morale, the feeling of security and invincibility, contributes largely to success. Offensives successfully executed over enemy territory quickly establish the spirit of victory and turn possible timidity into aggressiveness.

The particular method of attack which offers greatest probability of success is ordinarily pointed out by the leader's actions. Parallel attacks head-on, from rear or side, give no advantage to either adversary; the importance of gaining the upper position has already been emphasized and is to be remembered as a fundamental tactical rule. When attacking with the superior force the enveloping formation is frequently used; circling about the enemy, the airplanes engaged thus gain concentration of fire and lessen the chances for escape of the quarry. Pursuit is a matter almost entirely dictated by the superiority of speed. Here again higher altitude offers the advantage of speed acceleration in descent. Once it is determined that the pursued cannot be overtaken before the radius of action is exhausted, or the chase continued to dangerous depth over hostile territory, a return should be made. The escaping plane will generally fly directly toward the sun or into clouds or haze; there is also a fair probability that when nearly overtaken its pilot will suddenly slow down and drop, in an endeavor to have the pursuer pass him, thus reversing the situation.

Convoying bombing airplanes is an important duty of combat machines. Generally, the bombers leave the ground first, the swifter machines following some minutes later and meeting at the designated air rendezvous about the same time. The post of the fast fighters is above or on the flanks of the formation, flying as advance, flank and rear guards.

Fig 4.10a A successful attack on the enemy's tail from the rear and slightly below, an effective method when the attacking airplane has superiority of speed.

Fig 4.10b Maneuvering for position in air combat above the clouds.
From paintings by Lieut. Farré

CONTACT PATROL

A tactical reconnaissance during the progress of an attack, establishing a liaison between infantry of the first line and their commanders in the rear, giving positions of friendly and enemy troops, and carrying out offensive actions against enemy troops on the ground that is contact patrol, perhaps the most thrilling task that comes to the aviator in line of duty.

Airplanes assigned to contact patrol duty arrive over the front line trenches exactly at the time when the attack is scheduled to commence, taking a position just over or under the predetermined trajectory for the artillery barrage fire. The progress of the attack is observed; when the infantry advances to its first objective, its position is signaled to the aviators by means of a shutter, lamp or flare. The position is traced on the pilot's map, which is placed in a weighted message bag with any necessary comment; he flies then to the infantry headquarters, and coming down within 200 feet of the ground drops the bag. Sometimes the airplane's message is delivered in telegraph code by lamp, Klaxon horn or Very's lights and smoke bombs; wireless is occasionally used, but offers the possibility of interception by the enemy and is less desirable. The reports preferably include the state of enemy trenches during the attack, troop movements and location of any new trenches.

The offensive action, which is part of the object of a contact patrol, is literally a trench raid conducted in formation by combat aircraft. The usual method is for the first man to fly along the line of the enemy's first-line trench, very low under the barrage, in fact usually less than 100 feet above the trench parapet. The second man takes the second, or support line, both directing downward a stream of infilade fire from machine guns. It is the object of the second man to prevent effective fire at the first-line man; the airplanes in consequence fly almost abreast. Meanwhile, the support, or third line trench has been covered by a third airplane, with the object of demoralizing the troops in its shelter. A fourth airplane is meanwhile zig-zagging over the trenches, combating any attempts to direct effective rear fire from the trenches after the machines have passed.

The speed of flight of all four machines is 120 miles an hour or better, eliminating the possibility of accurate aiming by gunners returning small-arms fire from the trenches. Anti-aircraft guns are also ineffective at the low angle. The density of the air at the ground and the powerful types of airplanes used make the effect of wind puffs or disturbances from shell bursts negligible on control. The low altitude and high speed also tends to make the airplane rise; to overcome this the nose is pointed slightly downward, pointing the rigid gun at the best angle to rake the trenches.

When the machine guns have been discharged a return to friendly lines is made, a dangerous proceeding, as it requires flying up through the barrage fire, the smoke from which screens the craft from friendly gunners.

ARMOR FOR AIRPLANES

Armor, mounted in sheets protecting the airplane's vital parts, or in the form of turrets and shields, proof against small-arms fire, is indispensable and practical for low altitude operations. Armor plate ⅛ inch in thickness weighs about 10 pounds to the square foot, making the weight consideration an important one. The protection, therefore, is generally limited to armor plate beneath the motor and cockpit, disposition and quantity being governed by the type of airplane and the height at which it is usually flown. Protection from overhead fire not being considered, adequate security from rifle and machine gun fire on vital portions is thus gained by an average armored area of 30 square feet, or by an additional weight of 300 pounds. Flying efficiency being lessened by weight additions, the heavy armor protection which would be effectual against artillery fire is eliminated from calculations, leaving the evasion of fire to the airplane's high speed and maneuvering ability.

Turrets and shields are furnished for protection in combat with hostile airplanes, shields being mounted on universal joints so they can be lowered for underneath protection when not required by the gunner.

HEAVY AIRPLANE ARMAMENT

Explosive shells to be fired from airplanes have been successfully adapted to a specially designed, light weight 3-inch rapid fire gun. By reason of the short ranges used, high muzzle velocity is not required in air combat and the great weight of the same calibered field artillery piece may be cut down by elimination of the long barrel, recoil mechanism and heavy carriage. These aerial guns in consequence weigh less than 250 pounds. Instead of employing hydraulic cylinders for the recoil, the aviation arm takes up firing stresses by balanced fire, the gun having divided barrels, the projectile being loaded in the forward barrel, the powder charge placed in a chamber between it and a second barrel which is loaded with fine shot. When the

Fig 4.11 British Official Photo
Crew of an anti-aircraft battery securing ranging data.

gun is fired the fine shot is discharged backward, its force balancing in large measure that of the projectile discharging in the opposite direction. The slight difference in force is the recoil. Wooden breechblocks which blow out rearward are also used.

Heavy aircraft armament is used on airplanes of the super-plane class where lifting capacities of 4 tons are usual. The 3-inch and 2-pounder airplane guns do not have the high accuracy of fire which is essential to field artillery pieces and given by their higher firing velocities. Accuracy and high striking velocity is of less importance against aircraft, for the reason that high explosives can cause the collapse of an airplane without actual contact with it.

ANTI-AIRCRAFT FIRE

The most common trap which the aviator falls into is in diving to low altitudes over hostile territory and coming within range of anti-aircraft batteries. These dives may be occasioned by following an enemy airplane downward in heat of combat, or seeking to escape from a larger hostile air force. Deliberate luring of airplanes to altitudes within range of anti-aircraft fire is also a regular practice in warfare. Attacks on balloons and bombing expeditions on enemy bases also subject the military flier to this defensive fire from the ground. An understanding of anti-aircraft guns is valuable.

ACTION UNDER FIRE

The aviator under attack observes the effect of range fire directed at him by the white smoke of the shell bursts, termed "cream puffs." When the sound of the burst can be heard above the noise from his airplane motor it may be accepted that the gunners are getting the range with dangerous accuracy. An escape is then, in order. If diving or climbing is attempted the gunner may lower or raise his fire and estimate the airplane's velocity with fair accuracy. Perhaps the best method of escape is to employ the pancake, throttling the motor and dropping several hundred feet; this maneuver is difficult of detection from the ground, as the machine remains horizontal to its original position. Zig-zag flight ahead at high speed is then usually employed, although the straight course is a valuable variation because of its unexpectedness. All forms of aerobatics are frequently used when the shells are dangerously close.

Anti-aircraft artillery loses its accuracy of aim when the airplane is at elevations greater than 9,000 feet, although a chance hit may be expected. Shrapnel is less dangerous than high explosive shelling as a hit from its scattered fire must strike a vital part to be effective; explosive shells do not necessarily have to reach the target, however, as the light structure of a wing may be crushed by detonation in a near vicinity. The principal object of anti-aircraft fire is to force the airplane to greater altitudes, and while the percentage of hits is relatively small, the guns are sometimes amazingly effective at low elevations and the aviator's safety lies in climbing out of range.

LOCATION AND TYPES OF GUNS

Both fixed and mobile anti-aircraft artillery is well concealed by pits and camouflage from hostile airmen. The guns are of two types; important positions are usually defended by high power guns on fixed emplacements of concrete; the principal, and largest class, comprise light rapid-fire pieces, 1, 1½ or 2-pounders, and heavier types up to 6-pounders mounted on motor trucks of a special type. The heavy guns are generally used at headquarters of commanding generals of army corps, the lighter types being assigned to

Fig 4.12 Mobile anti-aircraft guns mounted on motor trucks.
British Official Photo

brigades and divisions in the field. While highly mobile, the guns are usually placed at supporting distance, about 1,000 yards apart. They have high muzzle velocity and consequent long range, firing projectiles with combination percussion and time fuses, explosive and incendiary charges. Automatic sights are used with graduated altitude, drift and deflection scales designed for high angle fire, 45 to 75 degrees. Fire correction is obtained by use of special projectiles giving off varying densities of smoke.

SHELL TRAJECTORIES AND BALLISTICS

The trajectory, or path described by a projectile, is influenced by gravity and time or resistance of the air. In anti-aircraft firing the line of sight is at angles up to 90 degrees and seldom less than 15 degrees, consequently the trajectory is unsteady and can only be aided in comparatively small degree by high velocity. Velocity losses as high altitudes are reached also serve to magnify small errors in aiming, which in turn are liable to frequent occurrence because of the short time allowed for computations.

A further contribution to inaccuracy is found in the changes in air density as altitude increases, affecting the ballistics of the shell. Time fuses for this reason burn erratically, wide variations in rate making them unsatisfactory;

the frail nature of the airplane mitigates against the operation of percussion fuses also, even though the projectile pass directly through the target. The percussion type does not explode unless it reaches its target and is therefore valueless for furnishing firing data.

Firing by salvo is considered the best method, four guns being arranged in a square at 200-foot intervals with the observer in the center. They are all aimed with the same firing data, a bracket being thus obtained on which corrections are based.

DEFENDING POSITIONS

Aviators must not underestimate the danger from anti-aircraft fire; improvements are constantly being made and the exercise of proper caution is required, particularly in raiding defended positions.

Outpost detector stations may be expected, equipped with microphones and other forms of electrical sound amplifiers which detect the approach of hostile aircraft at considerable distances. Telescopes and long range glasses sweep the skies constantly and powerful searchlights, fixed and mobile, are ready at night to throw a revealing beam on the invader. The outpost stations are also equipped with anti-aircraft batteries and combat airplanes which take to the air at the first warning of an enemy approach.

The line of interior defense ordinarily extends in a circle of four-gun groups placed at 1,000-yard intervals on a diameter of five or more miles from the defended position. These defenses must be passed before the objective is reached, when a fierce fire and engagement by combat craft may also be expected.

ATTACKS ON BALLOONS

Captive balloons used for observation and regulating artillery fire are most dangerous to attack. These helpless-appearing gas bags are about 200 feet long by 30 feet diameter, placed about 2 miles apart at an altitude of 4,000 feet. They are protected by several fast combat airplanes which circle above them, and an attack means flying through a heavy anti-aircraft barrage as well. Amazing accuracy is often attained by anti-aircraft gunners at the 4,000-foot altitude and the best are assigned to balloon protection.

One of the most successful methods of attack is for the hostile airplane to fly beyond the balloon's position at a minimum altitude of 6,000 feet, circling back over it and diving with the motor cut off, so it cannot be heard.

The dive for 1,500 feet should be steep with the machine in almost vertical position then slightly lessening the angle so a raking fire may be delivered when within 200 feet. If the tracer bullets show the mark has been reached, the attacker should swerve in a wide arc to avoid the effects of the explosion. After delivering gun fire quick climb is usually required to avoid the pursuing airplane guards and the shelling from the ground.

ENEMY AND "ACES"

The following chapter, although from a US publisher, is actually a translation of a French document written by one Oscar Ribel, Chief Instructor in one of the French military flying schools. It provides a useful comparison of French and German tactics and technology, albeit one skewed a little by the natural patriotism of the writer. The author references Georges Guynemer, one of France's top fighter aces with 54 victories. Guynemer began his career in the French Air Service in 1914 as a mechanic, but managed to force his way into pilot training and thereafter active service. In combat he proved himself an exceptional flyer and fighter. His technical feedback from the frontline also had an effect on aircraft design, specifically on the development of the SPAD XII and SPAD XIII. Guynemer was killed in action during a dogfight against unequal odds near Poelkapelle on 11 September 1917.

Textbook of Military Aeronautics (1918)

CHAPTER V   THE FUNDAMENTAL PRINCIPLES OF AERIAL COMBAT

The fifth arm has taken a very important part in the European war. The warmest advocates of military aviation in times of peace never dreamed of the vital importance of the aeroplane today.

In 1907 the most remarkable aerial flights were no farther than 1 kilometer, or ⅝ths of a mile, at a height of 30 meters, about 100 feet. The marvelous accomplishments in aviation during the last ten years are astounding. The most optimistic prophecies did not anticipate one half the actual reality. Who dared to believe, when Farman timidly tried his wings at Issy-les-Moulineaux, that nine years later escadrilles of thirty or forty aerial

Fig 4.13 The "Loop" as an aerial military manoeuvre. Attacked by four or five German machines, a French biplane turned completely over and returned by means of "looping the loop" to attack the squadron which was attacking him in the rear.

warriors would sail off into space to engage in heroic aerial combat against each other.

Aerial fighting has given an opportunity to develop in both the French and English rare qualities of courage, coolness, and hardihood. The Germans, on the other hand, are less well trained and equipped than their adversaries but, as is frequently recorded, exhibit undeniable bravery. The system used in aerial fighting differs in the German and Allied forces. In France we have distinct types of aeroplanes for different purposes, that is to say, for reconnoitering, "spotting" or directing artillery fire, and for carrying bombs. All these aeroplanes are protected by an escort of machines especially adapted for speed and fighting, and they are well armed. The Germans use their machines more indiscriminately for these various military operations. They do not have so many types of machines, and thus those they have are capable of being used for different purposes with equal efficiency. An exception to this statement are the Fokkers and the Walvets, which are flown by their most expert aviators and are used exclusively for fighting the enemy.

From a technical point of view French aviation is about the same as German, but our pilots are superior scientifically to the Germans, and the

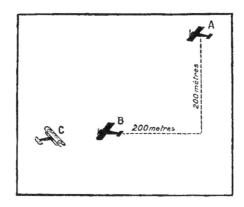

Fig 4.14 The favorite attack of the Walvets. Walvets patrol two by two. A 200 meters above and 200 meters behind B. If a machine C is encountered B engages in combat with it while A remains to survey the zone of battle to prevent surprise on the part of another machine which might come up to render assistance.

number of our "aces" is constantly increasing. Practically all of them fly the Nieuport or Spad, and their victories up to date can be numbered by the hundred. Naturally we cannot describe the methods employed by each one of these "aces" in fighting the enemy, because almost every one depends upon the marvelous individual skill with which they perform their acrobatic feats. One example among thousands may be quoted. It is well known among escadrilles at the front and will give an idea of how every pilot must cut the "Gordian Knot."

In the course of a reconnoitering flight in the East, sub-Lieut. Navarre found himself surrounded by five or six German machines. Three or four were above him and the others were below or at the sides, which prevented him from going to the right or to the left, either in rising or descending. It seemed impossible for him to escape. Without losing for an instant his remarkable coolness, our valiant "ace" surprised his adversaries by making a complete loop over the entire group of assailants, and following up the nearest machines, discharged an entire belt of cartridges from his machine gun and brought down two machines one after the other. The other pilots retreated as fast as possible to their lines, pursued by the intrepid Navarre.

The German "aces" are much less numerous than our own, the best among them being Captain Boelke, who died the 28th of October, 1916, after having brought down his fortieth adversary. We count as victories for our pilots only the enemy machines which fall inside our lines, or fall in flames in unoccupied territory, but the Germans do not hesitate to count every machine which is brought down for one cause or another, and is thus obliged to abandon the fight. If we adopted the same method of counting, it is certain that Guynemer, among others, has brought down more than sixty enemy machines. French aviators often fight twenty or thirty kilometers behind the German front. A German reconnoitering party must be checked in its operations and brought down if possible. During the course of our offensive on the Somme and at Verdun, our machines established a veritable barrier across our front, through which no German aviator was able to penetrate; and this lasted for several days.

Speed and climbing ability are essential for a fighting machine, as the aviator has to outfly his adversary and strike him in a vital spot at an opportune moment. The Fokkers, the Walvets, and the L.V.G. are the principle types used for reconnoitering over the front, and have a speed of 150 kilometers per hour (about 100 miles). They climb very rapidly, and the altitude at which aerial combat is generally fought is about 4000 meters (14,000 feet).

Generally speaking, the German fighting pilots, especially those who fly the Walvets, employ the following tactics when they come over our lines and engage our aviators. They always go in groups composed of units of two machines each. If an enemy machine is engaged by one of these units, the first of the German aviators begins the battle and the second man remains about two hundred meters above, his mission being to overlook the zone of combat without interfering directly with the fighting. If a second adversary comes to the rescue, however, it is his turn to attack and drive away the rescuer, while if his partner is vanquished, he returns to his lines as quickly as possible. Often the manoeuvers are more involved, and the aviators fly in large squadrons for mutual protection. If an isolated enemy is encountered, he is quickly surrounded and must seek safety in the speed of his flight.

The speed of the fighting machines is great, and there is danger therefore of breaking the wings. A machine which flies at 180 kilometers an hour (about 110 miles), rises two thousand meters in seven minutes (about 7000 feet),

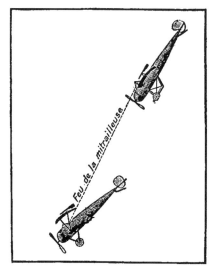

Fig 4.15 The "Dive Attack." To train the machine gun upon its target below the machine must be pointed down at least 60 degrees.

and dives almost vertically from this height, experiences a tremendous strain which, in time, is apt to cause weakness. Fighting machines have to perform extraordinary feats in pursuing the enemy. They dive vertically, and if the wings break under the pressure caused by these conditions, the machine at once falls. German machines, generally speaking, have a good factor of safety in their different parts. Many accidents have been caused after a machine has had many repairs, or through some hidden fault of construction. Recently at the front near Verdun an aviator was pursuing a German machine and, in his turn, was pursued by a small Rumpler biplane. At the moment when the French pilot, after bringing down his first adversary, was preparing to face this new assailant, the Rumpler dived straight toward the earth in a sudden bold dash. The wings broke and folded up above the fuselage. Many Rumpler machines have met the same fate in other air battles. The constructors thus involuntarily contribute to the success of our pilots, and thereby deserve our thanks.

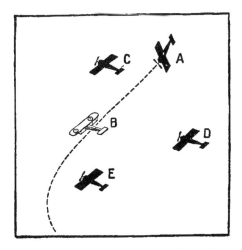

Fig 4.16 The tactics of the famous Boelke. The duty of the machines C, D, E, is to surround their adversary B at a given moment. A, who has been hidden from the view of his adversary, dashes at him, firing his machine gun furiously.

The German "aces" generally fight in conjunction with a squadron of accompanying machines. These are charged with the duty of occupying the attention of the enemy until an opportune moment for attack. Boelke adopted the following tactics, as described by M. Jacques Mortane. The German flew with an escadrille of five or six good pilots on Rolands, Walvets, or Fokkers; he preferred a Fokker, but sometimes was seen on a Roland, or a small Aviatik. As soon as the well-known profile of an Allied machine was seen on the horizon, the squadron rose to engage it. The duty of Boelke's support was to surround the enemy and block his path. They would fire from all sides, suddenly ceasing the instant Boelke made his entrance upon the scene. The latter would dash at his prey and attack furiously, firing a thousand cartridges from his machine gun. Boelke followed up the fight, in contrast to the custom of many of his compatriots. These rarely continued an engagement with an adversary who was not brought down at the first shot. Such was the method adopted by Lieut. Immelmann, one of the best of the German aviators. He would dash up to an enemy's machine, and when so close that a collision seemed imminent, would discharge his machine gun at it as he passed by. Once out of range he would not return to the attack, but would fly away, which cannot be considered very heroic.

The Germans usually fly very high. When they see French machines they hesitate to cross our lines, which are always well guarded by our fighting machines, especially during the periods of Allied drives. The weather plays an important role in air fighting. Calm days, when the sky is full of dark, gray clouds, are the most favorable for surprise attacks. The clouds act as a screen and allow the aviator to hide until the last moment, before he makes a dash at an unsuspecting enemy.

The Germans are well versed in one trick which they invented and which they have often used. When the bank of clouds is thick, one of their machines flies down to an altitude of two or three hundred feet. This machine may be of any class, but it is usually a slow machine of an old type, and not heavily armed. It appears to be relatively easy prey, and is quickly discovered by the French machines. They give chase, not hesitating to follow it, even to some distance behind the German lines. At the moment when the French pilot finds conditions most favorable to begin his attack, three or four German fighting machines of the latest and most formidable model appear. Flying above the clouds, they have been following the two antagonists while hidden from view, and never appear until the enemy is at least twenty or thirty kilometers from his base. The number of attacking machines, and the difficulties in getting help in time, make it an extremely precarious predicament for the French aviator.

An air battle does not necessarily end by the complete destruction of an enemy machine, or the killing or disabling of a pilot. A case has occurred where a German aviator was attacked by a French "ace." The German was convinced that he had no chance, lost his nerve, and preferred to come down in safety to having his body riddled with bullets. He directed the observer with him to throw up his hands, while he steered his captured machine, and following his vanquisher to the nearest aviation field, landed by the side of his captor. In this way Lieut. Laffon gathered out of a clear sky a Fokker of the latest model, and brought it to the aviation center of Plessis-Belleville. The feat was all the more remarkable and creditable to the officer because he had no arms aboard, except a revolver.

Before the war the question of arming machines received only superficial study, at least in France. At the beginning of hostilities only a few aeroplanes

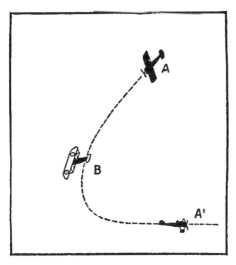

Fig 4.17 The tactics of Immelman. The machine A dashes straight at its enemy B, firing at him furiously. If he failed to bring down his prey he fled and did not return to the charge.

were equipped with machine guns. Many of the aviators had only a rifle with which to defend themselves against attack. Today, as the enemy well knows, our machines are very efficiently armed for both attack and defense. The position of a machine gun on the aeroplane plays a great part in the success of air fighting. We know that the Germans have studied the problem with great care, and their machine guns are mounted in one of the five following positions:

(1) Above the upper plane (machine guns stationary, firing through the propeller).

(2) Along the fuselage (gun stationary, shooting through the propeller).

(3) In rear of the lower plane (guns movable in a revolving turret).

(4) In front of the cockpit (gun movable and able to fire in all directions; single-motored machine with a pusher propeller).

(5) Both in front and in rear of the cockpit (gun movable; twin-motored machine, tractor propellers, with a central cockpit).

The first arrangement has been adopted by several manufacturers of small speedy biplanes in Germany, and is similar in almost all points to

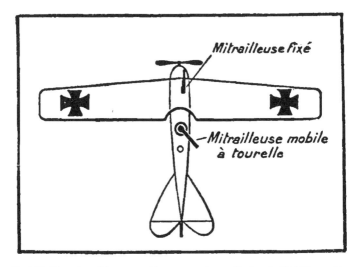

Fig 4.18 Mounting of the two machine guns on the new bi-plane L. G. V. The machine gun in front shoots through the propeller and is fired by the pilot. The rear gun mounted in a revolving turret is fired by the observer.

the system used on our Nieuports. The machine gun is stationary on the upper plane, parallel with the fuselage, and is controlled by a "Bowden" flexible wire control fastened to a rod beside the pilot. To train the gun upon its mark in the vertical plane one must point the aeroplane up or down; and to aim in the longitudinal plane, the aeroplane must be pointed in the direction of fire, since the gun is firmly mounted on the axis of the machine.

When the aeroplane attacked is just below the pursuing machine, the latter must dive vertically and attack its adversary while inclined at ninety degrees, in order to bring the machine gun into range. In practice, the angle of attack is not quite as steep as this, for the attacked machine is not exactly beneath its adversary's gun. It is at least 100 meters (300 feet) away, and when the attacking machine opens fire, it is at an angle of 55 or 65 degrees. This, when compared with the horizontal, is a considerable angle. The difficulty of hitting the mark is great, since the gunner and his

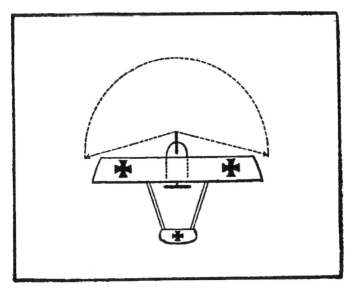

Fig 4.19 Arrangement of a machine gun with a limited field of fire. The gun is mounted in front of the car on an elevated support. The field is limited by the extremities of the aeroplane.

object are moving rapidly, and the movements in steering an aeroplane are complex and relatively slow. The mounting of the gun on the upper plane is best adapted to the machine which has the pilot's seat behind the wings. Consequently, to gain the best chance to reach the aviator himself, his adversary must strive to attack from above.

The mounting of guns for firing through the propeller was first attempted by Roland Garros, who was taken prisoner before he was able to destroy his machine. The Germans were quick to copy this method of mounting guns, and have made many improvements, as it was well adapted to the Fokker machine and gave very good results. On the Fokkers, the gun is mounted stationary above the hood, a little to the right of the axis, on a level with the head of the pilot. The propeller causes only slight inconvenience, but on account of the gun being firmly fixed, the entire

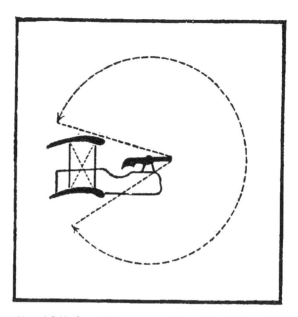

Fig 4.20 Vertical field of a machine gun mounted on a pivot. In the vertical plane the fire is very extended. It is only limited by the parts of the aeroplane.

machine must be aimed, with the attendant difficulties already mentioned. It is also possible to shoot through the propeller by using an automatic device to momentarily stop the fire during the passage of the propeller-blade in front of the gun. The latter is mounted directly behind the propeller. In this device the motor is connected with the machine gun, and a cam controls a mechanism which stops the fire for $\frac{1}{200}$ of a second, while the blades of the propeller are in the path of the bullets. When the propeller has passed, the gun is free to fire again. If a pilot wishes to shoot, he presses a small lever placed on the steering post, which is connected to the trigger of the gun.

The company licensed to make the Nieuports in Italy recently invented a device which enables one to shoot through the propeller, practically identical with that used on the Fokker. It is based on the difference between the speed of the gun and the speed of the propeller; that is to say, the ratio between the bullet and the propeller-blade is 700 to 160. This difference is used to regulate the stopping of the machine gun during the passage of the blade of the propeller in front of the barrel of the gun.

The arrangement which Garros used was extremely crude. It consisted simply of a small piece of steel, hard enough to resist a bullet, placed on each blade of the propeller opposite the barrel of the gun. If a bullet chanced to hit the propeller, the metal deflected it without causing damage to the propeller-blade. The German biplanes, like the L.V.G., for example, have two machine guns. One is stationary on the upper plane, the other movable and mounted on the fuselage behind the observer's seat, on a revolving turret. This gives it a great range of fire. The turret is a ring of wood which turns freely around the cockpit on ball-bearings, with a bracket arm which holds the gun and permits it both to be trained in the vertical plane and swung around in the horizontal plane to either side of the fuselage, so as to point in any direction. Two small clamps hold the turret and gun firmly in any position.

This arrangement gives a wide range of fire toward the rear in all directions, and on either side, both above and below. It is even possible to fire ahead, above the wings of the machine. The rear machine gun is often replaced by a "fusil mitrailleuse," or automatic rifle. To protect the blank sector of this gun arrangement, the fuselage is provided with a tube-like opening, inclined at an angle of forty-five degrees. This tube allows the gunner to see and fire through the fuselage at the enemy, if he tries to hide from view of the gunner below the rear of the machine.

The machine guns, when mounted in front and rear, are both fired by the observer, but in a recent type the forward gun was placed between the two planes beside the motor and parallel to it, being fired by the pilot. At the beginning of the war some German machines had a cockpit, like the French Farmans, with a gun mounted on an elevated support.

This mounting left a large blank sector of fire, and was afterward abandoned. The gun did not have much sweep, and its zone of fire was restricted by passengers, wings, propeller, cables, struts, etc. This was remedied in a measure by mounting it on a turret, which allowed it to fire in all directions, but not at all angles. This type of machine is not used today at the front. It has been replaced by the A. G. O., which is provided with two motors and tractor propellers, and a central car armed with two machine-gun turrets.

One machine gun is placed forward, sweeping the horizon for 180 degrees and the other is in the rear, its range also controlling 180 degrees of the horizon. Between them the entire horizon is covered. All of the German machines are armed with one or two Maxims, Lewis, or Parabellum machine guns. Some aeroplanes have three machine guns, and these are considered the best for actual service. The Parabellum has a belt of cartridges which contains not less than a thousand projectiles.

If each pilot has his own method of fighting, each type of machine has its weak points; and these points must be well known, in order to make a successful attack upon it. When attacking a machine it is necessary to learn how its guns are mounted, in order to know whether to attack it from above, below, or from the side. If the field of fire of the machine gun has certain dead

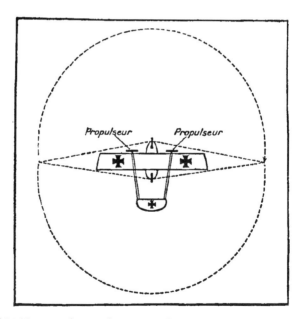

Fig 4.21 Mounting of two machine guns in a bi-motored machine. The arcs of fire in the horizontal plane meet each other when the guns are mounted in this manner.

points, it is thereby handicapped, and may be attacked to advantage. A pilot who is attacked by an Aviatik is exposed to fire from all directions, except in the zone in front of the propeller. In the case of ordinary Aviatiks, with the gunner in front, the machine gun can be placed at will on the right or left side of the fuselage. It is placed upon a pivot mounted on a carriage. This carriage can be moved on two guides, or slide bars, that run along the fuselage to a convenient point for firing. A clamp holds the carriage at any spot, so that one can fire in all directions. An aviator who attacks an L. V. G. which, as we have explained, has two machine guns, must decide whether it is better to stay in front or in the rear of the line of fire between the forward and the rear gun.

Thus we see that the identification of the type of enemy aeroplane is absolutely necessary for an air warrior. Unfortunately, the diversity of types of machines employed by the Germans, and the frequent changes made in service, renders this identification extremely difficult.

COLONEL OSWALD BOELKE

Oswald Boelke, mentioned in the previous manual extract, served in the *Luftstreitkräfte* from 1911 until his death in action on 28 October 1916. Boelke not only became an ace in his own right, with 40 air combat victories, but was also one of the true formative influences in the German air force in terms of its tactical evolution – even the great Manfred von Richthofen was one of Boelke's students. Boelke understood that victory in the air war was not just a matter of individual prowess, but it also of coherent and aggressive formation flying, with victories achieved through cooperation and cunning. He also formulated the *Dicta Boelke*, a list of eight rules for air combat. They were in summary:

1) Try to secure advantages before attacking. If possible keep the sun behind you.

2) Always carry through an attack when you started it.

3) Fire only at close range and only when your opponent is properly in your sights.

4) Always keep your eye on your opponent and never let yourself be deceived by ruses.

5) In any form of attack it is essential to assail your opponent from behind.

6) If your opponent dives on you, do not try to evade his onslaught but fly to meet him.

7) When over the enemy's line never forget your own line of retreat.

8) For the Squadron: Attack on principle in groups of four or six. When the fight breaks up into a series of single combats take care that several do not go for one opponent.

Boelke kept a field diary listing his exploits, and after his death this was translated and published into English, being widely read by Entente pilots as a form of instructional manual. Tactical information was not entirely standardised and shared in the RFC and Aéronautique Militaire until late in the war, so any sources of information were avidly digested, even if they did originate with the enemy.

An Aviator's Field Book, Being the Field Reports of Oswald Boelcke, from August 1, 1914, to October 28, 1916 (1917)

June 30, 1915
Rain, almost continuously, since the 22d. I am absolutely sick of this loafing.

Since June 14th, I have a battle-plane of my own: a biplane, with 150-horsepower motor. The pilot sits in front; the observer behind him, operating the machine gun, which can be fired to either side and to the rear. As the French are trying to hinder our aerial observation by means of battleplanes, we now have to protect our division while it flies. When the others are doing range-finding, I go up with them, fly about in their vicinity, observe with them and protect them from attack. If a Frenchman wants to attack them, then I make a hawk-like attack on him, while those who are observing go on unhindered in their flight. I chase the Frenchman away by flying toward him and firing at him with the machine gun. It is beautiful to see them run from me; they always do this as quick as possible. In this way, I have chased away over a dozen.

July 6, 1915
I succeeded in carrying a battle through to complete victory Sunday morning. I was ordered to protect Lieutenant P., who was out range-finding,

from enemy 'planes. We were just on our way to the front, when I saw a French monoplane, at a greater height, coming toward us. As the higher 'plane has the advantage, we turned away; he didn't see us, but flew on over our lines. We were very glad, because lately the French hate to fly over our lines. When over our ground the enemy cannot escape by volplaning to the earth. As soon as he had passed us we took up the pursuit. Still he flew very rapidly, and it took us half an hour till we caught up with him at V. As it seems, he did not see us till late. Close to V. we started to attack him, I always heading him off. As soon as we were close enough my observer started to pepper him with the machine gun. He defended himself as well as he could, but we were always the aggressor, he having to protect himself. Luckily, we were faster than he, so he could not flee from us by turning. We were higher and faster; he below us and slower, so that he could not escape. By all kinds of manoeuvers he tried to increase the distance between us; without success, for I was always close on him. It was glorious, I always stuck to him so that my observer could fire at close range.

We could plainly see everything on our opponent's monoplane, almost every wire, in fact. The average distance between us was a hundred meters; often we were within thirty meters, for at such high speeds you cannot expect success unless you get very close together. The whole fight lasted about twenty or twenty-five minutes. By sharp turns, on the part of our opponent, by jamming of the action on our machine gun, or because of reloading, there were little gaps in the firing, which I used to close in on the enemy. Our superiority showed up more and more; at the end I felt just as if the Frenchman had given up defending himself and lost all hope of escape.

Shortly before he fell, he made a motion with his hand, as if to say: let us go; we are conquered; we surrender. But what can you do in such a case, in the air? Then he started to volplane; I followed. My observer fired thirty or forty more shots at him; then suddenly he disappeared. In order not to lose him, I planed down, my machine almost vertical. Suddenly my observer cried, "He is falling; he is falling," and he clapped me on the back joyously. I did not believe it at first, for with these monoplanes it is possible to glide so steeply as to appear to be falling. I looked all over, surprised, but saw nothing. Then I glided to earth and W. told me that the enemy machine had suddenly turned over and fallen straight down into the woods below. We descended to a height of a hundred meters and searched for ten minutes, flying above the woods, but seeing nothing. So we decided to land in a meadow near the woods and search on foot.

Soldiers and civilians were running toward the woods from all sides. They said that the French machine had fallen straight down from a great height, turned over twice, and disappeared in the trees. This news was good for us, and it was confirmed by a bicyclist, who had already seen the fallen machine and said both passengers were dead. We hurried to get to the spot. On the way Captain W., of the cavalry, told me that everyone within sight had taken part in the fight, even if only from below. Everyone was very excited, because none knew which was the German and which the French, due to the great height. When we arrived we found officers, doctors and soldiers already there. The machine had fallen from a height of about 1,800 meters. Since both passengers were strapped in, they had not fallen out. The machine had fallen through the trees with tremendous force, both pilot and observer, of course, being dead. The doctors, who examined them at once, could not help them any more. The pilot had seven bullet wounds, the observer three. I am sure both were dead before they fell. We found several important papers and other matter on them. In the afternoon my observer, W., and I flew back to D., after a few rounds of triumph above the village and the fallen airplane. On the following day, the two aviators were buried with full military honors in the cemetery at M. Yesterday we were there. The grave is covered with flowers and at the spot where they fell there is a large red, white and blue bouquet and many other flowers.

I was very glad that my observer, W., got the Iron Cross. He fought excellently; in all, he fired three hundred and eighty shots, and twenty-seven of them hit the enemy airplane.

August 11, 1915

Early August 10th the weather was very poor so that our officer 'phoned in to the city, saying there was no need of my coming out. So I was glad to stay in bed. Suddenly my boy woke me up, saying an English flyer had just passed. I hopped out of bed and ran to the window. But the Englishman was headed for his own lines, so there wasn't any chance of my catching him. I crawled back to bed, angry at being disturbed. I had hardly gotten comfortably warm, when my boy came in again — the Englishman was coming back. Well, I thought if this fellow has so much nerve, I had better get dressed. Unwashed, in my nightshirt, without leggings, hardly half dressed, I rode out to the camp on my motorcycle. I got there in time to see the fellows (not one, but four!) dropping bombs on the aviation field. As I was, I got into my machine and went up after them. But as the English had very speedy machines and headed for home after dropping their bombs, I did not get within range of them.

Very sad, I turned back and could not believe my eyes, for there were five more of the enemy paying us a visit. Straight for the first one I headed. I got him at a good angle, and peppered him well, but just when I thought the end was near my machine gun jammed. I was furious, I tried to repair the damage in the air, but in my rage only succeeded in breaking the jammed cartridge in half. There was nothing left to do but land and change the cartridges; while doing this I saw our other monoplanes arrive and was glad that they, at least, would give the Englishmen a good fight.

While having the damage repaired, I saw Lieutenant Immelmann make a pretty attack on an Englishman, who tried to fly away. I quickly went up to support Immelmann, but the enemy was gone by the time I got there. In the meantime, Immelmann had forced his opponent to land. He had wounded him, shattering his left arm — Immelmann had had good luck. Two days before I had flown with him in a Fokker; that is, I did the piloting and he was only learning. The day before was the first time he had made a flight alone, and was able to land only after a lot of trouble. He had never taken part in a battle with the enemy, but in spite of that, he had handled himself very well.

August 23, 1915

On the evening of the 19th I had some more luck. I fly mostly in the evening to chase the Frenchmen who are out range-finding, and that evening there were a lot of them out. The first one I went for was an English Bristol biplane. He seemed to take me for a Frenchman; he came toward me quite leisurely, a thing our opponents generally don't do. But when he saw me firing at him, he quickly turned. I followed close on him, letting him have all I could give him. I must have hit him or his machine, for he suddenly shut off his engine and disappeared below me. As the fight took place over the enemy's position, he was able to land behind his own lines. According to our artillery, he landed right near his own artillery. That is the second one I am positive I left my mark on; I know I forced him to land. He didn't do it because he was afraid, but because he was hit. The same evening I attacked two more, and both escaped by volplaning. But I cannot say whether or not I hit them, as both attacks took place over the French lines.

September 18, 1915

Lately, I have flown to the front every evening with Lieutenant Immelmann, to chase the Frenchmen there. As there are usually eight or ten of them, we have plenty to do. Saturday we had the luck to get a French battleplane and between us chase it till it was at a loss what to do. Only by running away did it escape us. The French did not like this at all. The next evening we went out peacefully to hunt the enemy and were struck right away by their great numbers. Suddenly they went crazy and attacked us. They had a new type biplane, very fast, with fuselage. They seemed to be surprised that we let them attack us. We were glad that at last we had an opponent who did not run the first chance he got. After a few vain attacks, they turned and we followed, each of us took one and soon forced them to volplane to earth. As it was already late, we were satisfied and turned to go home. Suddenly I saw two enemy 'planes cruising around over our lines. Since our men in the trenches might think we were afraid, I made a signal for Immelmann to take a few more turns over the lines to show this was not so. But he misunderstood me and attacked one of the Frenchmen, but the latter did not relish this. Meanwhile the second 'plane started for Immelmann, who could not see him, and I naturally had to go to Immelmann's aid. When the second Frenchman saw me coming he turned and made for me. I let him have a few shots so that he turned away when things got too hot for him. That was a big mistake, for it gave me a chance to get him from behind. This is the position from which I prefer to attack. I was close on his heels and not more than fifty meters separated us, so it was not long before I had hit him. I must have mortally wounded the pilot, for suddenly he threw both his arms up and the machine fell straight down. I saw him fall and he turned several times before striking, about 400 meters in front of our lines. Everybody was immensely pleased, and it has been established beyond all doubt that both aviators were killed and the machine wrecked. Immelmann also saw him fall, and was immensely pleased by our success.

June 2, 1916

On the 17th of May we had a good day. One of our scout 'planes wanted to take some pictures near Verdun, and I was asked to protect it. I met him above the Côte de — and flew with him at a great altitude. He worked without being disturbed, and soon turned back without having been fired at. On the way back, I saw bombs bursting at Douaumont and flew over to get a closer view. There were four or five other German biplanes there; I also noticed several French battleplanes at a distance. I kept in the background and watched our opponents. I saw a Nieuport attack one of our machines, so I went for him and I almost felt I had him; but my speed was too great, and I shot past him. He then made off at great speed; I behind him. Several times I was very near him, and fired, but he flew splendidly. I followed him for a little while longer, but he did not appreciate this. Meanwhile, the other French battleplanes had come up, and started firing at me. I flew back over our lines and waited for them there. One, who was much higher than the rest, came and attacked me; we circled around several times and then he flew away. I was so far below him that it was hard to attack him at all. But I could not let him deprive me of the pleasure of following him for a while. During this tilt, I dropped from 4,000 meters to a height of less than 2,000. Our biplanes had also drifted downward.

Suddenly, at an altitude of 4,700 meters, I saw eight of the enemy's Caudrons, I could hardly believe my eyes! They were flying in pairs, as if attached to strings, in perfect line. They each had two engines, and were flying on the line Meuse-Douaumont. It was a shame! Now, I had to climb to their altitude again. So I stayed beneath a pair of them and tried to get at them. But, as they were flying so high and would not come down toward me, I had no success. Shortly before they were over our kite-balloons they turned. So fifteen or twenty minutes passed. Finally I reached their height. I attacked from below, and tried to give them something to re- member me by, but they paid no attention to me, and flew home. Just then, above Côte de —, I saw two more Caudrons appear, and, thank goodness, they were below me. I flew toward them, but they were already across the Meuse. Just in time, I looked up, and saw a Nieuport and a Caudron coming down toward me. I attacked the more dangerous opponent first, and so flew straight toward the Nieuport. We passed each other firing, but neither of us were hit. I was only striving to protect myself. When flying toward each other, it is very difficult to score a hit because of the combined speed of the two craft. I quickly turned and followed close behind the enemy. Then the other Caudron started to manoeuver the same way, only more poorly than the Nieuport. I followed him, and was just about to open fire when a

Fokker came to my aid, and attacked the Caudron. As we were well over the French positions, the latter glided, with the Fokker close behind him. The Nieuport saw this, and came to the aid of his hard-pressed companion; I in turn followed the Nieuport. It was a peculiar position: below, the fleeing Caudron; behind him, the Fokker; behind the Fokker, the Nieuport, and I, last of all, behind the Nieuport. We exchanged shots merrily. Finally the Fokker let the Caudron go, and the Nieuport stopped chasing the Fokker. I fired my last shots at the Nieuport and went home. The whole farce lasted over an hour. We had worked hard, but without visible success. At least, the Fokker (who turned out to be Althaus) and I had dominated the field.

On the 18th of May I got Number 16. Toward evening I went up and found our biplanes everywhere around Verdun. I felt superfluous there, so went off for a little trip. I wanted to have a look at the Champagne district once more, and flew to A. and back. Everywhere there was peace: on earth as well as in the air. I only saw one airplane, in the distance at A. On my way back I had the good luck to see two bombs bursting at M., and soon saw a Caudron near me. The Frenchman had not seen me at all. He was on his way home, and suspected nothing. As he made no move to attack or escape, I kept edging closer without firing. When I was about fifty meters away from them, and could see both passengers plainly, I started a well-aimed fire. He immediately tilted and tried to escape below me, but I was so close to him it was too late. I fired quite calmly. After about 150 shots I saw his left engine smoke fiercely and then burst into flame. The machine turned over, buckled, and burned up. It fell like a plummet into the French second line trenches, and continued to burn there.

On May 20th I again went for a little hunting trip in the Champagne district, and attacked a Farman north of V. I went for him behind his own lines, and he immediately started to land. In spite of this, I followed him, because his was the only enemy machine in sight. I stuck to him and fired, but he would not fall. The pilot of a Farman machine is well protected by the motor, which is behind him. Though you can kill the observer, and riddle the engine and tanks, they are always able to escape by gliding. But in this case, I think I wounded the pilot also, because the machine made the typical lengthwise tilt that shows it is out of control. But as the fight was too far behind the French front, I flew home.

The next day I again had tangible results. In the afternoon I flew on both sides of the Meuse. On the French side two French battleplanes were flying at a great altitude; I could not reach them. I was about to turn back, and was gliding over L'homme mort, when I saw two Caudrons below me, who had escaped my observation till then. I went after them, but they immediately flew off. I followed, and at a distance of 200 meters, attacked the one; at that very instant I saw a Nieuport coming toward me. I was anxious to give him something to remember me by, so I let the Caudrons go and flew due north. The Nieuport came after me, thinking I had not seen him. I kept watching him until lie was about 200 meters away. Then I quickly turned my machine and flew toward him. He was frightened by this, turned his machine and flew south. By my attack, I had gained about 100 meters, so that at a range of 100 to 150 meters, I could fill his fuselage with shots. He made work easy for me by flying in a straight line. Besides, I had along ammunition by means of which I could determine the path of my shots. My opponent commenced to get unsteady, but I could not follow him till he fell. Not until evening did I learn from a staff officer that the infantry at L'homme mort had reported the fall of the machine. In the evening, I went out again, without any particular objective, and after a number of false starts I had some success. I was flying north of Bois de —, when I saw a Frenchman flying about. I made believe I was flying away, and the Frenchman was deceived by my ruse and came after me, over our positions. Now I swooped down on him with tremendous speed (I was much higher than he). He turned, but could not escape me. Close behind the French lines, I caught up with him. He was foolish enough to fly straight ahead, and I pounded him with a continuous stream of well-placed shots. I kept this up till he caught fire. In the midst of this he exploded, collapsed, and fell to earth. As he fell, one wing broke off. So, in one day, I had gotten Numbers 17 and 18.

CHAPTER 5
AIR-TO-SURFACE OPERATIONS

The manuals featured in this chapter make a distinct shift in focus from the previous chapter. As much as World War I established and refined the art of fighter vs fighter combat, it also did likewise for a whole range of air-to-surface operations. The types of mission covered in this phrase can be especially broad, depending on where we draw the boundaries, especially if we include maritime aviation. They include artillery observation, close air support, strategic bombing, convoy escort and anti-submarine sorties. As each of these missions was formed more clearly, and resourced properly, it led to a proliferation of aircraft types designed to handle the specific tactical challenges. The aircraft ranged from modest but useful two-seaters such as the British Airco DH.4, which variously served in day-bombing, reconnaissance, anti-submarine and even night-fighter roles, through to monster bombers such as the Zeppelin Staaken R.VI, with its seven-man crew and a wingspan of 42.2m (138ft 6in). The ground-attack mission also saw the production of some innovative types, such as the German monoplane Junkers J 4, which had an all-metal construction to help it withstand the depredations of small-arms fire from the ground during low passes.

Three manuals are featured in this chapter, each concerning a different aspect of the working combat relationship between ground forces or a surface navy and the aviation services. The first of these manuals, *Instructions for the employment of aerial observation in liaison with the artillery* was produced in its original French version on 19 January 1917, and translated into English shortly thereafter for the American Expeditionary Force, such was its clarity and utility. In the passages provided here, we get a real sense of the technical understanding and the spatial awareness required by an effective aerial observer. For gunners on the ground, having an "eye in the sky" could make a fundamental difference to the precision and concentration of a barrage, and for the aviator, controlling the delivery of sometimes thousands of shells was an onerous responsibility.

Instructions for the employment of aerial observation in liaison with the artillery (1917)

PART I.

CONDITIONS GOVERNING THE EMPLOYMENT OF AERIAL ORSERVATION IN LIAISON WITH ARTILLERY.

1. Under good atmospheric conditions, the aeroplane can give rapid, accurate and, if necessary, vertical observation even on the most distant targets. It makes it possible to observe not only the sense of salvos, but also the amount of the observed error.

2. The aeroplane signals to the ground by means of wireless telegraphy, by projectors, by dropped written messages, or by signal lights. Wireless telegraphy is the best method. A conventional code, Morse system, permits the observer to report his presence to designate targets, to report results of fire, and to give all required information to friendly troops concerning the movements of the enemy. This information is received at the receiving stations described in paragraph 8 and 11.

3. The receiving stations can, by means of panels of white cloth or projectors, give the aeroplane a limited number of simple indications concerning the conduct of fire. There are in addition a few receiving sets on aeroplanes which can be used with transmitting sets at receiving stations near important headquarters.

4. Use of Wireless Telegraphy: The use of wireless telegraphy has given a tremendous importance to aerial liaison with artillery. On account of its delicate nature, and the great number of aeroplanes which necessarily have to work in a restricted zone, strict discipline and careful organization are necessary to reduce to a minimum the many chances for confusion.

Different aeroplanes are distinguished as follows:

a. By the «call» adopted for each receiving station.

b. By the use of varying wavelengths.

c. By varying the loudness of the emission.

d. By the use, in certain cases, of watches with colored dials which make it possible for neighboring aeroplanes to send their signals at alternate specified intervals and thus avoid confusing their signals. This device interferes with the continuity of observation and should be used only when necessary.

It is important that aeroplanes keep out of neighboring zones, and that they do not come closer than two kilometers to their own receiving stations except for very important messages. Messages sent when immediately above the antennae interfere seriously with other messages.

Technical matters concerning Wireless Telegraphy are prescribed in each Army, and in each Army Corps by the Chief of the Radio Service concerned. In each Army Corps designated officers of air-squadrons supervise the Wireless Telegraph Service in their own squadrons and at the receiving stations. These officers are under the orders of their squadron commanders and of the Chief of the Radio Service of the Army or Army Corps.

5. Projectors: By means of projectors communication can be established:

a. When the artillery has no receiving station.

b. When there are many aeroplanes working in one zone and interference amongst wireless messages is unavoidable.

c. When the distance is not too great.

d. Projectors of neighboring aeroplanes can be distinguished:

    1. By the orientations of sheafs of light, or

    2. By the use of a pre-arranged call.

6. Dropped Written Messages: Dropped written messages may be used to give information concerning targets or the results of fire. Each message is placed in a small container provided with a streamer. They should be dropped from a height not more than 300 meters and as close to the receiving station as possible.

7. Use of Signal Lights: In principle, signal lights are used only for communication with the infantry. During the artillery preparation, their use with the artillery may be authorized by proper authority. A conventional code must be adopted at a preliminary conference, and only a few simple messages can be sent.

8. Receiving Stations: Each Artillery Command, Sub-Command, or Group (in certain cases, each Battery) is equipped with a receiving station. A specially trained officer called the Receiving Officer [*officier d'antenne*] is provided at each receiving station. He transmits by voice or telephone to the unit concerned the interpretation of the information received from the aeroplane. It is an important and delicate duty requiring great specialization.

Each receiving station must have direct permanent telephone connection with each battery. In each artillery command there must be provision for the use of auxiliary receiving stations when the antennae at the main receiving stations are broken.

9. Telephones: Connections are provided as required by the Instructions on liaison.

10. Panels: Each receiving station is provided with identification panels which enable aeroplanes to distinguish their own receiving stations. They are especially necessary when the artillery changes position.

In addition to the identification panels, window-shutter panels [*panneaux à persiennes*) are provided for use with the Morse code.

All panels are transported by the artillery units to which they are issued.

11. Receiving Stations: The use of receiving stations varies with the tactical situation as follows;

a. The receiving station of a group or battery acts as a station for the adjustment of the fire of its own unit. (Note: A «group» corresponds to a field artillery battalion in the U.S. Service.)

b. The receiving station of an artillery sub-command acts as a post of commandment. The aeroplane asks such stations for authority to adjust on targets which appear in the zone and receives from such stations the orders of the artillery commander. In the case of special groups or batteries which have been given particular missions, the aeroplane consults the group or battery direct without the intervention of the artillery commander.

c. The receiving station of a command acts as fire control station. It follows the work of the aeroplanes of the Artillery Command as well as that of the infantry aeroplanes operating in the same zone in order to gather all important useful information.

d. **Supervising Receiving Stations** of each Army Corps are placed near the Corps Headquarters or else at Artillery Headquarters. They should, in general, receive messages from all the aeroplanes of the Army Corps or at least from all those having a general mission, such as supervising the artillery, accompanying the infantry or operating with the higher command. In this way, they receive and distribute all information sent in by the aeroplanes. Whenever it is evident that calls from aeroplanes are being disregarded or not being heard, supervising receiving stations will notify subordinate receiving stations.

e. **Receiving Stations at Air-Squadrons** Each air-squadron has a receiving station by which the emissions of aeroplanes may be verified at the moment of departure, the work of the aeroplanes at the front followed, and relief of aeroplanes requiring it may be furnished.

12. The Artillery Commander, after conference with the Air Commander and the Chief of the Radio Service of the Army Corps or the Army, fixes the conditions governing the work of the personnel at receiving stations.

At certain times, particularly during an action or in a war of movement, the Artillery Commander will provide for uninterrupted listening service at receiving stations in order that all aeroplanes calling the Artillery Command or Sub-Command may be put in communication at once. The complete liaison is the duty of the Receiving Officer (*officier d'antenne*). He should study it with care and be held responsible for the proper working of all means of communication (telephone, optical telegraph, wireless telegraph, messengers, etc.).

13. The signal codes for wireless telegraphy, for projectors, for identification panels and a model for dropped written messages will be found in Annex II.

BALLOONS.

14. Balloons usually observe at from 1,000 to 1,500 meters, never above 2,000. These altitudes must be reduced in strong winds. Balloons with two baskets can carry two observers with separate telephone connection.

15. On account of its vulnerability, the balloon must keep at a long distance from the enemy, not less than 9,000 to 10,000 meters when ascents, descents, etc., have to be made. Once in the air, it can be carried on the winch to within 6,000 or 7,000 meters.

16. There are always portions of the terrain hidden from the balloon observer. Such dead spaces will be marked on the map and furnished to the Artillery Commands.

17. On account of the delay involved in changing observers, during action an observer must remain up all day.

18. The telephone is depended upon for communications. The necessary lines are shown in the Instructions on liaison. In addition, each Balloon Company is furnished with a wireless telegraph sending set with which information received from the balloon may be sent to the Higher Command and the Artillery Groups in cases in which the telephone connection is interrupted.

19. Mobility: When the way is not blocked by trees, wires, etc., balloons can be easily moved without denotation or even when in the air.

PART II.

ARTILLERY MISSIONS WHICH AERIAL OBSERVATION CAN ASSIST.

20. Such missions are:

Artillery Information covering enemy works in a sector;

Observation of enemy activity in a sector;

Liaison with other Arms;

Observation and Adjustment of artillery fire.

21. Artillery Information Service: This consists in obtaining all possible information concerning enemy works so that the following targets may be located:

Posts of Command, machine-gun emplacements, battery positions, communication trenches, etc. Photographs, interpreted by specialists, are superior to information furnished by the observer himself. After details have been located in photographs, however, a second personal reconnaissance, made with high-powered field-glasses, will often be of value.

22. All aerial information gained by an air squadron is consolidated by the Information Officer of the Squadron who communicates it at once to the Artillery Information Officer (S. R. A. — *Service Renseignements d'Artillerie*). In a similar manner, the Artillery Information Officer of a Command transmits all his information to the Air Service.

Targets are identified by giving their co-ordinates. Each enemy, battery thus identified should be described on its own information card.

From photographs, the rough sketches by the Air Service, the Corps Provisional Interpretations, and the Firing Maps are made up. The rapid transmission of these sketches, especially during an action, is of the greatest importance.

23. The Observation Service consists in watching a given sector for the purpose of giving immediate information in regard to active batteries in order that friendly troops in danger may be warned, and eventually the action of friendly troops be observed.

24. Such service is particularly hard on aeroplane observers for, on account of the noise of their own motors, they can hear nothing and must watch uninterruptedly. For this reason, aeroplane observation is carried on only over terrain hidden from the balloons or during action.

25. Except in cases of zones defiladed from balloons and for special missions, aeroplanes will not be used for continual observation except when no balloons are available.

26. The service of continual watchfulness should be developed. It is the duty of the aerial observer to call for immediate fire whenever he may judge it necessary. It is the duty of the Commanding Officer to see that troops co-operate with aerial observers. If possible, receiving stations will notify aerial observers as to which battery is going to fire.

27. Liaison with Infantry or Cavalry: This is covered by Instructions on liaison.

28. Observation of Fire: This service includes the following:

Fire for adjustment or verification, in order to register the terrain and prepare for fire for effect;

Fire at a single range and fire of precision for the purpose of neutralizing or destroying the enemy's works;

Systematic fire opened by shifting a previously established sheaf of fire in order to neutralize momentarily targets upon which fire of precision cannot be undertaken.

29. The sense and amount of errors in firing can be given only if each salvo or rafale is fired at the demand of the aerial observer. For adjustment of fire and for fire for precision, the aerial observer is particularly suitable. He increases the efficiency of fire and saves ammunition. For systematic fire when the aerial observer is not advised before the firing of each salvo or rafale, aerial observation is of less value.

30. Aerial observation is limited to three hours at most and is liable to interruptions due to atmospheric conditions or aerial combats. For this reason, battery commanders should fire as rapidly as their materiel permits without sacrificing accuracy to speed.

The balloon which is useful at short or mid ranges as it communicates easily with the ground is also useful for certain adjusting fire and fire of precision. It is sometimes useful to open fire which the aeroplane finishes, and inversely to observe fire for effect which the aeroplane has commenced.

[No. 31 missing]

32. Co-ordination of Service of Balloons and Aeroplanes: This co-ordination is realized as follows:

By a judicious division of duties between aeroplanes and balloons, on the part of the Artillery Commander;

By the close association of the two services, inter-communication by means of documents, plans, photographs, and good telephone service connecting the squadrons and balloons of the same command. This assurance of this association is the duty of the Air Commander of the Army.

33. Division of Duties among Aeroplanes: Whenever an aeroplane can be assigned to each Artillery Command and the artillery preparation has been partially made, each observer should be given a definite task of observation and of fire in his own zone.

In order to avoid errors, observers who have identified targets should ordinarily be required to adjust fire on those same targets when possible.

But, under certain other conditions, it may be advisable in a large zone to assign to one aeroplane the supervision and control of systematic fire and to others the adjustments and the fires of precision.

34. The relative importance of the different missions assigned to aeroplanes varies with circumstances and the various phases of the action. It is indicated by the Commanding General.

35. However, in an offensive action against a fortified position the chief missions to be given to artillery aeroplanes follow one another as follows:

a. Information service and observation service in order to determine precisely the location of enemy batteries and positions.

b. Observation for the registration of the terrain and the adjustment of batteries on the principal targets on which they can fire.

c. Observation of fire for precision for the destruction of enemy batteries and defensive positions.

d. Observation for fire control commencing as early as possible on the day of the attack.

e. During the action, neutralization or destruction of enemy's batteries, dispersion of reserves and reinforcements, and watchfulness over well-defined zones for the observation of fire for effect and for rapid shifts to new targets particularly important. It may even be necessary to assign such targets to special aeroplanes.

36. Periods of Movement: In principle, in periods of movement, each division is given its zone of march and action. This zone is explored by aeroplanes. In accordance with plans made in advance, they communicate the information obtained by aerial signal lamps, by signal lights, or by wireless telegraphy to information centers established successively along the route of the Division according to the orders of the Division Commander in such a way that reception shall be continuous. Such information centers are in communication with the aviation field by optical telegraph, telephones, wireless telegraphy, pigeons, aeroplanes and automobiles.

At each information center there must be an officer of the Air Service who should at once select a landing ground easy of access, and near the information center. The Commanding General at once details the necessary personnel for the observation and establishes all means of liaison possible.

The Division Commander has the Artillery Commander with him and successively moves his headquarters from one information center to another as the advance continues. The Artillery Commander makes requests on the Air Service, through the information center, for such aeroplanes as he may require, assigns them to his units and indicates their missions if possible.

Upon leaving the squadron, the aeroplanes fly towards the information center which at once indicates the groups to which they have been attached and the targets concerned. The groups indicate their positions by displaying their panels.

Artillery Division and Group Commanders must establish receiving stations whether they are needed at once or not. For this purpose, the wireless telegraphy tractors are pushed as far forward as possible. Landing grounds should be near information centers. The Divisional Artillery Commander sends the necessary orders to the landing grounds, and when possible retains observers who utilize such aeroplanes as come in to the landing grounds for the carrying out of new missions which may be given them. In no case should lack of landing grounds or telephonic communication interfere with aerial observation. As the fight develops, conditions more and more approach those of stabilized or trench warfare.

ANNEX I

PART I.

RULES FOR THE CONDUCT OF FIRE.
AEROPLANES WITH LIGHT ARTILLERY.

1. Aerial observation permits exact reconnaissance of targets, the measurement of errors in deflection and range, the observation of rafales or salvos delivered simultaneously and the measurement of their mean error.

The difficulties include precarious communication, the short time available for observation, the rapid movement of the aeroplane, snow, wind, rain, clouds, the sun, ground hidden by the wings and the limited action of the wireless telegraph. All of these difficulties render aerial observation at times intermittent.

Success implies a close understanding between the observer and the battery commander, the use of simple means of communication, and the avoidance of all dialogue. Great latitude should be allowed the aerial observer in making requests, decisions, etc. The battery commander should avoid loss of time by being able to adjust quickly once he has received the proper information.

CONDUCT OF FIRE.

2. In service firing there should always be a preliminary conference between the observer and the battery commanders, but for practice this conference should frequently be omitted.

Before passing to aerial conduct of fire, it is the duty of the battery commander:

a. To adjust the sheaf;

b. In time-fire, to adjust the height of burst just above the ground;

c. To adjust all his guns for range on an auxiliary target visible for terrestrial observers;

d. To establish a direct line of communication to the receiving station, avoiding all relays.

Assuming that this has been done the aerial observer, after reaching the required height sends his call and signals as follows:

Observer: *Is the Battery ready?*
Receiving station: *The Battery is ready.*

3. Adjustment of Fire: It is assumed that, unless otherwise agreed upon or requested, all firing shall be by battery salvos adjusted for parallel fire. To vary the distribution, the observer sends for example:

Front n *meters. — Sheaf is too wide.*

For registration on a narrow target, the observer sends, for example:

Concentrate. — Fire otherwise good.

4. Battery salvos are fired with all guns at the same range and as nearly simultaneously as possible.

5. In principle, the same ammunition which is to be used in fire for effect should be used in fire for adjustment; but, in principle, it is desirable to use time-shrapnel for preliminary adjustment of the deflection on account of its greater visibility. If the height of burst must be changed to avoid a cover, it must be changed with the angle of site and not with the corrector in order to keep all bursts in the same vertical plane.

6. Fire should be always delivered when the aerial observer asks for it. If there is to be a delay of more than thirty seconds, do not fire but wait for another request from the observer. Interruptions of a serious nature are signalled by one of the following messages:

Wait several minutes, or

Battery not ready. — There will be a delay of more than ten minutes. No farther need of you.

7. It is essential that the preliminary adjustment be as accurate as possible. Frequent correction of the deflection, etc., wastes too much valuable time. If the observer, when in a position to observe, sends:

Lost,

do not fire again with the same data, but use data half way between that of the last salvo seen by the aerial observer and the salvo which he has been unable to see. But, on the contrary, if the observer sends:

Was not in a position to observe,

the previous data should be repeated.

8. Errors in range are reported by taking the average error of the four shots of the salvo with reference to the target. Errors in deflection are reported by taking the interval between the right of the sheaf and the right of the target. Before obtaining proper bracketing, the battery must make corrections as required by reported errors. In difficult country where bursts are hard to observe, the aerial observer should ask for rather conservative corrections.

9. To correct a sheaf badly distributed, the aerial observer may send, for example:

No. 1. — Fire.

The first gun then fires two rounds rapidly. By causing the first and fourth guns to fire, the front of the sheaf may be ascertained.

10. To shift the sheaf to a new target, or to a new part of an old target, the aerial observer should send, for example:

Change Target. — Add 200.

11. Fire for Effect: This may be either fire for precision at a single range, each volley or salvo being observed by the aerial observer and the adjustment being constantly refined, or it may be zone fire.

12. When firing at a single range, battery volleys of two or four rounds each are usually employed. Each volley is fired at the request of the aerial observer who reports the mean error of each. Concentrated fire is very easily observed and is useful for this reason.

13. Fire for Precision by single Piece: The aerial observer may send, for example:

No. 4. — Fire for Precision. — Fire.

No. 1. then fires four rounds at full speed, and the aerial observer reports the mean error of the group of bursts.

14. Zone Fire: This may be either:

a. After the aerial observer has completed adjustment and observed the delivery of more or less prolonged fire for effect. In an action, this observation is usually restricted to the observation of the limits of a 100-yard bracket. For this, the aerial observer demands, for example: *Zone fire*, or

b. Progressive Fire, which is usually delivered after adjustment on a target or an auxiliary target, without verification.

Only the general effect can be reported. The zone to be covered should usually not exceed 100 meters.

BOMBING ACCURACY

The practice of aerial bombing was one of the topics addressed in the *Textbook of Military Aeronautics*. In the short passage reproduced here, the author explains some of the complexities involved in actually putting bombs onto target, and not just in the general vicinity. The sheer number of factors that affected bombing accuracy was extensive, involving numerous complexities in physics and mathematics. These factors included the airspeed, direction, altitude and attitude of the aircraft; the general direction and speed of the wind; humidity, temperature and other atmospheric effects; visibility over the target; the weight and shape of the bomb; the bomb-release mechanism; whether the target was protected or not; and anti-aircraft resistance at the target site. Little wonder, therefore, that the accuracy of bombing, particularly from high altitudes, had a margin of error measured in the hundreds of metres.

Nevertheless, there were accuracy improvements during the war, not least in the development of bombsights. The purpose of a bombsight was to remove some of the burden of human estimation from the targeting equation. For example, the Drift Sight, developed by Henry Wimperis, and introduced into the Royal Naval Air Service (RNAS) in 1916, mechanically measured the surrounding windspeed and made a calculation of how this affected the fall trajectory of the bomb (previously the bombardier had to rely on the use of a stopwatch and mental arithmetic). Numerous other types were produced and incorporated, and gradually bombing became less a matter of guesswork. In some RFC raids of 1918, for example, bombing aircraft were able to put bombs consistently on or around individual trains in marshalling yards. Yet as World War II would continue to demonstrate, bombing from altitude remained an imprecise business, and would be so for many decades.

Textbook of Military Aeronautics (1918)

CHAPTER III

DROPPING BOMBS FROM AEROPLANES

By Jean-Abel Lefrance

Last February a French aviator, Captain Guynemer, succeeded in bringing down inside the French lines, one of a raiding squad of 20 German bombarding planes of the newest type, manufactured by the Gotha Wagonen Fabrik. A peculiarly interesting feature of the aeroplane was its Goerz sighting telescope or range-finder, designed to facilitate the taking of correct aim at objects to be bombarded. A careful study of this, with a discussion of the laws governing the dropping of bombs, appears in "La Nature" (Paris), together with the accompanying diagrams.

Any projectile dropped from a height is subject, of course, to two constant forces, the resistance of the air and the acceleration due to gravity. Its trajectory is a vertical line from the point of discharge. A, to the striking point, B (5.1a). If the bomb be dropped from an airship in motion, it will have an initial speed equal to and in the same direction as that of the latter. This new force is compounded with the two former, and the result is the curved trajectory A C.

If this bomb, having a given initial velocity, is dropped into a layer of air in motion, that is, into the wind, it is acted on by the latter, and is said to undergo "drift." If the wind is at the back, the trajectory is lengthened, as in A D; if there is a head wind, the trajectory will be shortened, as in A E.

If the bomb be dropped from an avion which the strength of the wind causes to be stationary' with respect to the ground, i.e., when the

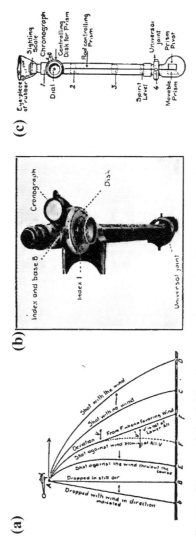

Fig 5.1 a. Trajectory of a bomb falling from an aeroplane as affected by the direction of the wind.
b. The Goerz range-finder.
c. Diagram showing construction of the Goerz range-finder.

velocity of the wind is exactly equal to that of the avion and in the opposite direction, the projectile will have no initial velocity and the curve of its trajectory will be a function solely of the drift produced by the wind, as in A *b*; it will therefore fall to the rear of the point of departure. This latter case, however, is exceedingly rare, since it presupposes a wind of 120 to 150 kilometers per hour; but this is a gale too high to permit the sending up of aviators.

These trajectories being given, the angle of aiming will be the angle formed by the vertical line A V at the point of departure A with the straight line joining this point A with the striking point O, i.e., the angle VAO.

Since these trajectories are curves, the height of the avion above the object aimed at is an element which modifies the value of the trajectory. Since wind causes drift, this drift will vary with the form of the projectile and with the velocity of the fall. Here we have two elements which are constant for each type of bomb.

To sum up, the trajectory of a bomb discharged from an avion is the resultant of the following forces:

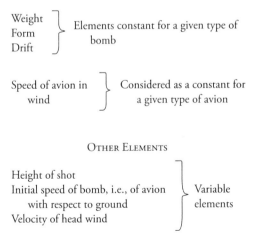

Weight
Form
Drift
⎫ Elements constant for a given type of
⎬ bomb
⎭

Speed of avion in
wind
⎫ Considered as a constant for
⎬ a given type of avion
⎭

OTHER ELEMENTS

Height of shot
Initial speed of bomb, i.e., of avion
with respect to ground
Velocity of head wind
⎫ Variable
⎬ elements
⎭

Of these three principal variable elements which it is necessary to know for each case of bombardment, one of them, the velocity of the head wind, can be immediately deduced when the velocity of the avion with reference to

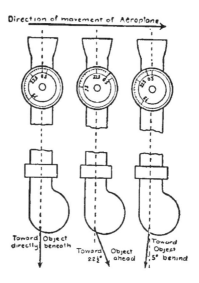

Fig 5.2 Direction of aim in the finder.

the earth is known, since this velocity of the wind is the difference between the velocity of the avion with respect to the earth and its normal velocity in the wind, an element which is fixed for a given type of avion.

Take an avion having a normal speed of 150 km. per hour; if it is only going 100 km. per hour with reference to the earth, then it is flying against a head wind of 50 km. per hour. Hence it is only necessary to know the height of the avion and the initial speed of the bomb to determine a trajectory. This method of calculating trajectories seeks to base itself on science in order to obtain a mathematical precision in its results. Unfortunately it is based upon a probable knowledge of atmospheric conditions, which are essentially capricious. Particularly, the speed of the wind at the height of the avion is taken into account, e.g., at 4000 meters, but it is supposed that this remains unmodified down to the ground, which is rarely the case in reality. It may also be that, starting from 3000 meters, the wind changes its direction so much that the best calculations, the best telescopes, and the best bombardiers, are unable to secure a correct aim, so that some authorities despair of ever being able to get results in aerial bombardment comparable to the efforts made.

NAVAL AVIATION

Naval aviation was a specialist sub-set of military flying, and one in which Britain – that most maritime of nations – made a particularly heavy investment. The Royal Naval Air Service (RNAS) was formed in January 1914, and initially grew quicker in scale than the RFC, with more than 300 aircraft by the beginning of the war. By April 1918 it had some 67,000 officers and men, 2,949 aircraft, 103 airships and 126 coastal stations. Aviation offered huge potential for naval and merchant operations, with the aerial platform providing a superb vantage point for observation of huge expanses of seascape and a mobile response to surface and underwater threats. Hence the RNAS main duties were coastal patrols, maritime reconnaissance, convoy escort and anti-ship/submarine missions, although it also flew bombing missions against ground targets and flew fighter missions over the Western Front. The text below is from the manual *Notes on the Cooperation of Aircraft with Surface Craft for Escorting Convoys of Merchant Ships*, which was published in 1918. It provides particular detail about the practice of submarine hunting, which the RNAS pursued with both fixed-wing aircraft and airships. Although air power's role in actually destroying the U-boat threat was limited, both official and historical analysis suggests that the aircraft did have a definite deterrent effect upon the submarine operations.

***Notes on the Cooperation of Aircraft with Surface Craft for Escorting Convoys of Merchant Ships* (1918)**

PART II.

INSTRUCTIONS TO PILOTS AND OBSERVERS WORKING WITH CONVOYS.

1. **In bright sun,** seaplanes escorting convoys should take station so as to be **between the sun and the convoy.**

The reason for this is that it is easier to observe from the seaplane with the sun behind, and it is harder to be seen yourself.

This applies equally to submarines, which, if possible, attack from the sunny side so that the periscope may be hidden by the glitter of the sun's reflection in the water.

A further advantage to the seaplane from taking up this position is that if a submarine, in a position between you and the convoy, tried to locate you in his periscope, you will probably locate him through the reflection of the sun in the lens.

In taking up station abreast of convoy, remember that a submarine will not attack at a greater range than about 3,000 yards and will endeavor to put in a shot at a range very much less.

2. **If the weather is dull and the wind is light,** say, 5–10 miles per hour, the seaplane should **carefully watch the lee side,** and keep near the convoy.

The reason for this is that, with these conditions, a submarine will try to get into position to fire a shot from the stern tube at a ship in the convoy on the lee side, since in this position she will be moving slowly away from the convoy, more or less ahead of the seas, thus making very little spray.

3. **In a strong breeze,** seaplanes should direct their most careful attention **to the weather side.**

Submarines attack, if possible, from the weather side in a strong breeze, since it is harder to keep watch from a ship on the side where the look-out man has the wind in his eyes.

4. **In a perfectly flat calm a submarine is not likely to attack a convoy except from the sunny side.**

The feather of the periscope is easily seen in calm water but practically invisible in the flitter of the sun's reflection.

5. With a wind about 10–15 miles per hour, as strong a seaplane escort as possible should be provided, and observers should keep a specifically sharp look out, **wearing submarine goggles all the time.** These will make the periscope show up bright red.

The weather conditions are the most favourable to submarines. If the periscope is shown sparingly, the sea just washes over it without masking the view and at any considerable distance the periscope feather, seen from a ship, cannot be distinguished from small breaking seas.

6. If the sea is rough it is possible that a submarine will not attack a convoy unless it is proceeding head or stern to sea.

Under these conditions, unless a torpedo is fired at right angles to the sea, it will break surface.

7. In a heavy sea, or a long Atlantic swell, a submarine will not usually attack.

8. When the sea is calm and the visibility good, with a slow convoy (6–8 knots), seaplanes should search about 10 miles on either side and ahead, as a submarine may possibly be on the surface about 15 miles away, observing the masts and smoke of the convoy, and taking bearings in order to get into a position to attack later in the day.

A submarine seen under these conditions should be attacked so that he may be kept under until the convoy, having been warned, is out of striking distance.

A submarine will probably not take precautions to conceal himself until he is about 4,500 years from the convoy. With fast convoys it is only necessary to scout ahead.

A submarine cannot travel fast enough, excepting on the surface, to overtake a fast convoy, so that an **attack is only likely from a position ahead in which the submarine has been waiting.**

9. **When a submarine gets near a convoy she will use her periscope very sparingly, i.e., she will show it frequently, but only for a very short time and only a few inches of it.**

In some waters the wake of the periscope remains clearly defined on the surface in white foam.

If a seaplane should spot a periscope or its wake, he should immediately proceed to the position and stay about there till the next appearance, which will probably be very near the same place. He should fly as low as safety will allow, and be ready to drop his bombs, should the opportunity occur.

On the first sighting the periscope the surface escort will a once be warned.

If, however, the periscope has been sighted at less than 4,000 yards from the convoy, the seaplane should gradually work its way, from the position in which the periscope was last seen, towards the convoy, and then circle about on the side the submarine was last seen, as the submarine, having worked up to a convoy by showing tis periscope often and for short periods, may dive to about 60 feet, and then proceed submerged by reckoning to a position from which an attack may be made.

If, therefore, the seaplane takes up the position near the convoy as mentioned above, he may, with the aid of submarine goggles, succeed in spotting the periscope as the Submarine comes up to make the attack, and be able to get hits with his bombs before the Submarine has time to fire his torpedo.

Failing a hit, having called up the surface escort, it should at least be possible to drive the submarine off from the convoy.

10. If flights of gulls are seen hovering over some object in the water, a seaplane escorting the convoy should always go and see what the object is.

A submarine, proceeding with its periscope just awash, often attracts the gulls.

11. If, as sometimes happens, the first intimation of the presence of a submarine is either the explosion of a torpedo or the observation of its wake, bear in mind the follow points:—

(*a*) The torpedo was probably fired from 200–500 yards from the ship.

(*b*) The submarine will probably keep the periscope up long enough to observe the result of the shot and then dive to the greatest possible depth, steering a course away from the convoy at full speed in the direction of its stern.

(*c*) If no bombs or depth charges are dropped on the submarine, he will probably break surface again after about 15 minutes to have a cautious look around.

Acting on the above, the seaplane should proceed at full speed and as low as possible to the position in which he thinks the submarine is most likely to be found. He can judge of this from the track of the torpedo, or from the ship and the position in which it was hit.

If he spots the periscope and gets over it, he should drop both bombs and warn surface escort.

If he spots the periscope but submarine dives before he can get over it, he should reserve his bombs and circle about at a two-mile radius from the sport for half an hour, as the submarine will probably break surface again within that time if not attacked.

If no periscope is sighted the seaplane should still circle about the two-mile radius of the torpedoed ship for half an hour waiting for the submarine to come to the surface.

12. Remember that the closest communication should be kept between aircraft and surface craft employed on convoy work.

When you pick up a convoy, report by lamp to the senior ship of the escort, and remain under his order till you report that you are returning to base in accordance with previous orders.

If ships, not supplied with Aldis lamps, with to make a signal with searchlight to seaplane, the pilot should fly in a straight line away from the ship, in order to avoid as little training of the searchlight as possible, and to give the observer the best position for reading the signal.

Pilots and observers should be made to be thoroughly acquainted with all Very's Light Signals, etc., also recognition signals and marks, as used by British submarines and surface craft.

Position relative to Submarine that Bombs should be dropped.

Notes from R.N.A.S. Anti-Submarine Report, No. 7, Dec., 1917:—

13. The following information as to the probable distance of a submarine ahead of the swirl of the propellers is promulgated for the guidance of Officers of R.A.F. (Naval) Stations, from which hostile submarine patrols are carried out.

Assuming that:—

1. Swirl appears 80 feet abaft the propellers,
2. Point to aim at is 80 feet before the propellers,
3. Submarine submerges at six knots, *i.e.,* 10 feet per second,

it appears that:—

2 seconds after submarine submerges bombs should be dropped

						180 ft. ahead of swirl	
4	”	”		”	200	”	”
6	”	”		”	220	”	”
8	”	”		”	240	”	”
10	”	”		”	260	”	”

Distance ahead of Oil or Bubbles that Bombs should be dropped.

OIL.

Speed of submarine or tide in knots	Depth of Water in feet at which submarine is lying or travelling.						
	25	50	75	100	125	150	175
2	71	141	212	283	354	424	495
3	106	212	319	425	531	637	744
4	142	283	424	566	708	849	990
5	177	354	531	708	855	1062	1239
6	212	425	638	850	1062	1275	1488

AIR BUBBLES.

	25	50	75	100	125	150	175
2	54	107	160	214	268	321	374
3	80	160	240	320	400	480	560
4	107	214	320	427	534	661	747
5	133	267	400	533	666	800	933
6	160	320	480	640	800	960	1120

Fig 5.3

EXAMPLE:—Suppose submarine to be lying on bottom in 75 feet of water, tide 3 knots. Then, under "75" and opposite "3" will be found number of feet, viz.:—319 feet, which represents the distance ahead of oil showing on surface it is necessary to drop a depth charge in order to render it effective.

Size of bomb required to render attack effective.

Considerable attention has been devoted to the question of limiting size of bombs which should be carried to ensure of the submarine being damaged and destroyed by the attack of aircraft.

Early in the year experience had shown that the weights of charge of the smaller sizes of bombs, 16 lbs., 65 lbs., and 100 lbs., are all insufficient, and that it was necessary to increase the charge considerably. This led to the adoption of the 230-lb. bomb, the first attack with which was carried out in June, 1917.

In estimating the weight of explosive required the following points are of interest:—

(1) Out of a total of four "known" cases of submerged submarines having been destroyed by depth charged the submarine has succeeded in reaching the surface again in three instances before finally sinking. This has not occurred in the case of aircraft attack, and seems to indicate that larger bombs than those yet used are required.

(2) There is an area of certain radius within which, say, 90 per cent, of the bombs dropped by patrol machines will fall. This area should diminish with increased practice and improved sighting instruments. Its radius is now taken as being 60–70 feet from the point of aim with flying boats of the America type.

(3) A charge, provided it is above a certain minimum size, will damage a submarine seriously when exploded in contact with the hull, and greater charges will produce similar damage at a distance from the hull.

NOTE:—A case has occurred in which a British submarine has returned to port after having her bow tubes wrecked by the explosion of a mine. The strength of a submarine's hull at the ends of the boat, both forward and aft, is very great, and in estimating the effect of an explosion near her, consideration must be given to the extent of the flat, or nearly flat, surface, on which the force of the explosion will be able to act.

(4) The object in view is to use such a charge that the figure which will be traced by the limiting distance from the hull described in (3) will coincide with the area discussed in (2).

See Figure 5.4 in which a bomb giving effective destruction power at 45 feet on the beam abreast the maximum diameter is hypothesised. The area of destructive range is probably somewhat as shown shaded. The conning tower is taken as the point of aim and a radius for 90 per cent. of hits as 70 feet.

Of bombs dropped within this radio 87½ per cent. should be effective, or about 80 per cent. of the total when allowance is made for 10 per cent. of really bad shots.

From the foregoing it will be seen that a bomb effective up to a distance of about 45 feet from the hull is required to give a reasonable prospect of a successful attack.

Experiments have been carried out and estimates made to determine the distance at which a charge of given size will destroy or seriously damage a submarine.

Figures such as the following have been given:—

40 lbs. of explosive at 10 feet.

120 lbs. of explosive at 35 feet.

300 lbs. of explosive at 70 feet.

It is feared that little reliance can be placed on any such estimates at present, and, taking into consideration the uncertainty of the depth at which the boat is diving, it is strongly recommended that the light case 520-lb. bomb should be carried whenever possible.

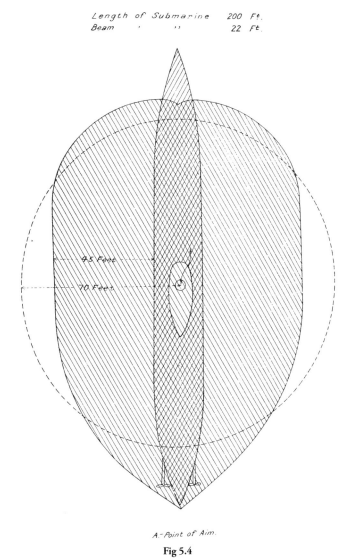

Length of Submarine   200 Ft.
Beam   ,,   ,,   22 Ft.

9.5 Feet

70 Feet

A.-Point of Aim.

Fig 5.4

SOURCES

CHAPTER 1 DOCTRINE

Military Aviation (US Army War College, 1943)

Offence versus Defence in the Air (General Staff, War Office, October 1917)

CHAPTER 2 TRAINING AND CORE FLYING SKILLS

Training Manual, The Royal Flying Corps, Part 1 (Provisional) (General Staff, War Office, 1914)

Textbook of Military Aeronautics, by Henry Woodhouse (The Century Co., 1918)

Learning to fly in the U.S. Army; a manual of aviation practice, by E.N. Fales (McGraw-Hill/Hill Publishing, 1917)

CHAPTER 3 AIRCRAFT ASSEMBLY, CARE AND REPAIR

Training Manual, The Royal Flying Corps, Part 1 (Provisional) (General Staff, War Office, 1914)

A Few Hints for the Flying Officer (Training Directorate, Air Ministry, Air Council, n.d.)

CHAPTER 4 AIR-TO-AIR TACTICS

Aeroplanes and Dirigibles, by Frederick A. Talbot (William Heinemann, 1915)

Practical Aviation, including construction and operation, by J. Andrew White (Wireless Press, 1918)

Textbook of Military Aeronautics, by Henry Woodhouse (The Century Co., 1918)

An Aviator's Field Book, Being the Field Reports of Oswald Bölcke, from August 1, 1914, to October 28, 1916, trans. by Robert Reynold Hirsch (National Military Publishing Co., 1917)

CHAPTER 5 AIR-TO-SURFACE OPERATIONS

Instructions for the employment of aerial observation in liaison with the artillery, trans. by Headquarters American Expeditionary Forces, Office of Chief of Air Service (Paris Imprimerie Nationale, 1917)

Textbook of Military Aeronautics, by Henry Woodhouse (The Century Co., 1918)

Notes on the Cooperation of Aircraft with Surface Craft for Escorting Convoys of Merchant Ships (Air Division, Naval Staff, 1918)